Do You Know the Muffin Man?

By Pam Schiller and Thomas Moore

Other books by the Authors:

Thomas Moore

Humpty Dumpty Dumpty by Thomas Moore

Where Is Thumbkin? by Pam Schiller and Thomas Moore

Pam Schiller

The Complete Book of Activities, Games, Stories, Props, Recipes, and Dances by Pam Schiller and Jackie Silberg

The Complete Resource Book for Toddlers and Twos by Pam Schiller

The Complete Daily Curriculum for Early Childhood: Over 1200 Easy Activities to Support Multiple Intelligences and Learning Styles by Pam Schiller and Pat Phipps

The Complete Book of Rhymes, Songs, Fingerplays, and Chants by Pam Schiller and Jackie Silberg

Creating Readers by Pam Schiller

The Practical Guide to Quality Child Care by Pam Schiller and Patricia Carter Dyke

Start Smart: Building Brain Power in the Early Years by Pam Schiller

The Complete Resource Book: An Early Childhood Curriculum With Over 2000 Activities and Ideas by Pam Schiller and Kay Hastings

The Values Book: Teaching 16 Basic Values to Young Children by Pam Schiller and Tamera Bryant

Count on Math: Activities for Small Hands and Lively Minds by Pam Schiller and Lynne Peterson

Sensitive Situations by Pam Schiller

Parties Kids Love: Great New Party Ideas for Birthdays, Holidays, or Just For Fun by Mike Artell and Pam Schiller

Rainy Day Recess by Pam Schiller and Mike Artell

Under Construction: Beginning Math by Pam Schiller and Lynne Peterson

Practices in the Early Childhood Classroom by Pam Schiller

The Earth and Me by Mike Artell and Pam Schiller

Where is Thumbkin? by Pam Schiller and Thomas Moore

The Instant Curriculum: 500 Developmentally Appropriate Learning Activities for Busy Teachers of Young Children by Pam Schiller and Joan Rossano

Children's Books

Sing a Song of Opposites by Pam Schiller

The Zebra on the Zyder Zee by Pam Schiller

Moncure, T. and Schiller, P. (2002) *This Old Man is Rockn' On*, Columbus, OH: SRA/McGraw-Hill.

Humpty Dumpty by Pam Schiller and Thomas Moore

Sara Sidney: The Most Beautiful Iguana in the Whole World by Pam Schiller and Tamara Bryant

A Chance for Esperanza by Pam Schiller and Alma Flor Ada

Roll-On, Roll-On by Pam Schiller

The Itsy Bitsy Spider by Pam Schiller

Books in Press

The Bilingual Anthology of Stories, Songs, and Fingerplays by Pam Schiller, Beverly Irby, and Lara Rafael-Alecio

The Complete Curriculum for Infants by Pam Schiller

The Instant Curriculum; Revised Edition by Pam Schiller and Joan Rossano

Literacy Activities Using
Favorite Rhymes and Songs

Do You Know the

Muffin Man?

An Essential Preschool
Literacy Resource

Pam Schiller
and
Thomas Moore

gryphon house, inc.
Beltsville, Maryland

Copyright

Illustrations: Deborah Wright and Richele Bartkowiak

Library of Congress Cataloging-in-Publication Information

Schiller, Pamela Byrne.
  Do you know the muffin man? / by Pam Schiller and Thomas Moore.
    p. cm.
  Includes index.
  ISBN 0-87659-288-4
  1. Reading (Early childhood) 2. Children's songs--Texts. 3. Early childhood education--Activity programs. I. Moore, Thomas, 1950- II. Title.
  LB1139.5.R43S37 2004
  372.41'4--dc22

                                                              2004004111

Bulk purchase

Gryphon House books are available for special premiums and sales promotions as well as for fund-raising use. Special editions or book excerpts also can be created to specification. For details, contact the Director of Marketing at Gryphon House.

Disclaimer

Gryphon House, Inc. and the authors cannot be held responsible for damage, mishap, or injury incurred during the use of or because of activities in this book. Appropriate and reasonable caution and adult supervision of children involved in activities and corresponding to the age and capability of each child involved, is recommended at all times. Do not leave children unattended at any time. Observe safety and caution at all times.

Table of Contents

Appendix

Indexes

Introduction

Songs, Chants, and Rhymes

Rhyme, rhythm, and music are essential parts of a quality early childhood curriculum. These play a role in setting the tone of the classroom, developing skills and concepts, helping children make transitions, and building a sense of community. Of course, if you ask the children, they will say that rhyming and singing are part of their daily activities because they're just plain fun!

Early Literacy Skills

In recent years, with a strong national focus on early literacy, we have begun to examine and define the valuable role singing songs and reciting chants and rhymes plays in laying the foundation for reading readiness. We know, for example, that singing songs and reciting chants and rhymes help build vocabulary and develop sound discrimination. The size of a child's vocabulary *(oral language)* and his or her skill in being able to discriminate sounds *(phonological awareness)* are strong predictors of how easily a child will learn to read when exposed to formal instruction. But oral language and phonological awareness are not the only skills that are developed when children are exposed to songs, chants, and rhymes. They also help develop listening and comprehension skills. With conscious effort, singing songs and reciting rhymes and chants can be used to provide opportunities for children to develop *letter knowledge and recognition* and to become familiar with the conventions of print.

Song, Chants, and Rhymes as a Springboard

Song, chants, and rhymes can be used to develop every aspect of reading readiness including disposition. In order for children to become avid readers they need to master the skills *(mechanics),* but they must also have the desire to read *(disposition).* Disposition grows from positive experiences. Singing songs and reciting chants and rhymes provide a natural way to build the development of reading readiness skills while ensuring the acquisition of disposition.

Do You Know the Muffin Man? is a collection of traditional songs, chants, and rhymes with suggestions for ways they can be used to support the development of

basic reading readiness *(literacy)* skills. Simply singing the songs and reciting the chants and rhymes with children is a great first step, but to capitalize on the full range of benefits inherent in using songs, chants, and rhymes as a springboard to literacy, they must be used intentionally as real learning opportunities. The activities suggested with the songs, chants, and rhymes in this book provide opportunities for enhancing the development of listening and oral language development skills, as well as opportunities for building comprehension skills, supporting print awareness, and refining the knowledge and recognition of letters.

Cross-Generational Links

Children should be introduced to songs, chants, and rhymes that span time. First, they need selections that are traditional—so traditional that their grandparents, even great-grandparents, will recognize them. This includes songs such as "Twinkle, Twinkle, Little Star" and "Yankee Doodle" and the poems and rhymes of poets like Robert Frost, Langston Hughes, and Laura Richards. Children also need to experience songs, chants, and rhymes that are modern traditional such as "Itsy Bitsy Spider," "Miss Mary Mack," and "Peanut Butter." These are selections that have words, tunes, or both that are familiar to their parents. Finally, children also need to have their own songs, chants, and rhymes—new selections that will someday be the classics of their generation. These might include "Sing a Song of Opposites," "Once There Were Three Brown Bears," "Humpty Dumpty Dumpty" and "This Old Man Is Rockin' On."

Songs, chants, and rhymes that span several generations help maintain threads of unity as a society, as a culture, and as a perspective on history. They tie us to tradition while respecting our evolution into the future. Songs, chants, and rhymes are markers for each generation—a way to say, "This is who we were." Some fond memories might include singing with your families—at church, around the piano at family gatherings, in the car, while you worked, maybe even singing to your new baby brother. Nothing is more fun and satisfying than singing together. Do you remember the first time you came home from school singing a song and your mother or father said, "Hey, I know that song!"

To provide this link for children, they need exposure to many songs, chants, and rhymes. The wider the breadth of that exposure, the greater their ability to see the threads that link us to one another. *Do You Know the Muffin Man?* embraces the concept of cross-generational music and rhymes and, although we hope children will have some exposure at home, we want to widen the exposure through the use of both familiar and new songs, chants, and rhymes in the classroom.

Regional Links

Songs, chants, and rhymes are also diverse when viewed from a geographical perspective. Not everyone in this country knows every song in this book. There are a few exceptions, but for the most part songs, chants, and rhymes are regional and sometimes even local. However, again, the wider the exposure the more likely children are to grow into adults who can sing their old favorite songs with any group of people from any age group and from any geographic location. The goal is to connect people one to another.

What Does Brain Research Say About Singing?

Singing makes us feel good, and when we feel good, our body releases endorphins into our system that will help boost our memory. Singing also requires that we take in additional oxygen, which increases our alertness. Singing is a great activity for enhancing brain functions.

Using This Book

There are more than 250 songs, chants, and rhymes in *Do You Know the Muffin Man?* The follow-up activities for each selection focus on using the song, chant, or rhyme to enhance the development of literacy skills. Because questions are a great way to stimulate both thinking *(comprehension)* and speaking *(oral language)*, we have included suggested questions to ask children in many of the activities. Stimulating discussions are a great way to build oral language and comprehension skills. This is an often overlooked opportunity for building literacy skills. The book also provides reflection questions to use at the end of each day. Research suggests that this is one of the best ways to help children process what they have learned.

Many of the songs, chants, and rhymes in this book include examples of different literary terms, including alliteration (when several words in a row have the same beginning letter and sound), onomatopoeia (a word that sounds like its meaning), and exclamations (words and phrases used to show emotion). Explain to the children what the terms mean, and point them out whenever they occur. (All literary terms appear in boldface type.)

Throughout this book, we present a variety of ways to help children practice writing some of the words from the songs, chants, and rhymes. Some children may be able to write many of the words. Therefore, we suggest letting each child make his or her own Word Box (shoebox with a lid). Let the children decorate them as

desired. Suggestions for words to practice writing are made throughout the book. If able, children can write the suggested words on index cards and keep them in their Word Box.

In the appendix you will find rebus recipes, patterns, and a list of words in American Sign Language to teach children.

Do You Know the Muffin Man? can be used to support your daily lessons or as stand-alone lessons. There is a theme chart (appendix p. 223) that provides a map for how the songs, chants, and rhymes might fit in with specific themes. This will help you use the selections as a support to the themes you are teaching. If you want to use the songs, chants, and rhymes as support to specific aspects of literacy, you can use the index. For example, if you are looking for activities to support the development of listening skills, simply look under "listening" in the index to find those songs, chants, and rhymes with specific suggestions for listening. You can do the same for oral language, phonological awareness, print awareness, comprehension, and letter knowledge and recognition.

The songs, chants, and rhymes in this book also make great transition activities. Print your favorites on index cards and keep them in your pocket. Take one out during transitions and watch it work its magic.

Keep the Joy

Please be careful not to over-teach lessons. Choose only one or two of the follow-up activities each time you use a song or rhyme. Do not lose the song or rhyme in the drill and practice of skills. Over-teaching lessons will turn children off and the joy of the song, chant, or rhyme may be lost to them forever.

Don't forget your own joy. Singing comes from within all of us and there is truly no such thing as a person who cannot sing. Singing is your internal voice of celebration and although you may not be a Pavarotti, Garth Brooks, Patti LaBelle, or a Barbara Streisand, you have a voice that is uniquely yours. If you claim you can't sing you will model that thinking for children. And by not singing, you send the same subtle message. No one should deny his or her joyful expression. We want all children to find their internal voice of joy. You are their guide. "Children... seem to have a clearer understanding of what constitutes a good voice. The children I know hear every voice for what it has to offer: Beauty. Power. A way for human beings to connect. The opening of a soul." [Moore, T. (2002, July). If you teach children, you can sing. *Young Children,* p. 84-85.]

When You Don't Know the Tune

There may be traditional songs in *Do You Know the Muffin Man?* that are unfamiliar to you. Familiarity with songs is determined by life experiences, geographic location, cultural background, family traditions, and a whole array of circumstances that may never be identified. What is so wonderful is that the great diversity of traditional songs created by these differences provides opportunities for us to continue to add new songs to our personal collections throughout our lives.

If you come to a song you don't know, look it up on one of the websites provided in the appendix (p. 241). Most sites provide an opportunity to actually hear the lyrics. If there is a song you can't find, say it as a chant or rhyme. The inherent value of the rhyme and rhythm will still provide a rich language experience for the children.

Learn While the Children Learn

One of the best things this book offers is the inherent opportunity within the songs, chants, and rhymes to help children enhance the development of early literacy skills. It can help you see a myriad of possibilities. It will also help you better articulate the value of singing and reciting chants and rhymes. With accountability knocking at the door of the classroom, it is critical to speak to the educational and learning value of these activities. This is a new era for all of us. The best way to grow with our profession is by experiencing firsthand the kinds of activities that can best guide the literacy journey for young children. There is no teacher like experience.

We know that you and the children in your classroom will enjoy the activities in *Do You Know the Muffin Man?* Singing and reciting chants and rhymes are just plain fun for all of us. You can't help but fall in love with language when you experience it with rhythm, cadence, rhyme, and melody. Keep a song in your heart and a poem in your pocket—they are great tools for developing a foundation for literacy!

The Alphabet Forward and Backwards

The Alphabet Forward and Backwards
(Tune: Twinkle, Twinkle, Little Star)

A – B – C – D – E – F - G,
H – I – J – K – L – M – N – O – P,
Q – R – S – T – U – V,
W, X, Y, and Z.
Now I know my ABC's.
Next time sing them backwards with me.

Z – Y – X – W – V – U – T,
S – R – Q – P – O – N – M – L,
K – J – I – H – G – F,
E – D – C, B and A.
Now I've said my ZYX's.
Bet that's not what you expected!

Related Songs, Chants, and Rhymes

Alphabet Boogie by Thomas Moore*
B-a-Ba, B-e-Be, B-i-Bi, B-o-Bo, Bi-Bo-Bu, I love you.
C-a-Ca, C-e-Ce, C-i-Ci, Co-o-Co, Ci-Co-Cu, I love you.
    **I Am Special CD, Thomas Moore Enterprises*

Alphabet Song (Tune: Twinkle, Twinkle, Little Star)
A – B – C – D – E – F - G,
H – I – J – K – L – M – N – O – P,
Q – R – S – T – U – V,
W, X, Y, and Z.
Now I know my ABC's.
Next time won't you sing with me?

THEME CONNECTIONS
Alphabet
Humor
Nursery Rhymes
School

Nursery Rhyme Rap (Tune: Ninety-Nine Bottles of Pop on the Wall)

Jack and Jill went up the hill

To get a pail of water.

Jack fell down and broke his crown

And Jill came tumbling after.

Oh, A B C D E F G...H I J K L...M N O P...Q R S... TUVWXYZ!

Humpty Dumpty sat on a wall

Humpty Dumpty had a great fall.

All the king's horses and all the king's men,

Couldn't put Humpty together again.

Oh, A B C D E F G...H I J K L...M N O P...Q R S...TUVWXYZ!

Little Miss Muffet sat on her tuffet

Eating her curds and whey.

Along came a spider who sat down beside her

And frightened Miss Muffet away.

Oh, A B C D E F G...H I J K L...M N O P...Q R S...TUVWXYZ!

Hey, diddle diddle, the cat and the fiddle

The cow jumped over the moon.

The little dog laughed to see such a sight,

And the dish ran away with the spoon.

Oh, A B C D E F G...H I J K L...M N O P...Q R S...TUVWXYZ!

Little Boy Blue, come blow your horn,

The sheep's in the meadow, the cow's in the corn.

Where is the boy who looks after the sheep?

He's under the haystack fast asleep.

Oh, A B C D E F G...H I J K L...M N O P...Q R S...TUVWXYZ!

Hickory, dickory, dock,

The mouse ran up the clock.

The clock struck one, the mouse ran down,

Hickory, dickory, dock.

Oh, A B C D E F G...H I J K L...M N O P...Q R S...TUVWXYZ!

Literacy Activities

(Select one or two follow-up activities to do each time you sing a song or say a rhyme.)

Oral Language Development

1.   Discuss the alphabet with the children. Explain that the alphabet is a family of letters that go together in a special order. Show them that letters are mixed up when they are used in words, but they are in order when they stay together as a family of letters.

2. Discuss the difference between forward and backward. Have a child demonstrate moving forward and then backward.

Letter Knowledge and Recognition

1. Point to the alphabet (alphabet wall cards) as you sing the song. Ask questions. *Which letter is the first letter of the alphabet? Which letter is the last letter in the alphabet? Which letter of the alphabet is the same as the first letter of your name?*
2. Place four consecutive alphabet cards on the floor. Ask the children to close their eyes while you remove one of the letters. When they open their eyes, can they tell you which letter is missing?
3. Read your favorite alphabet book. As you read about each letter, ask the children to indicate when the letter is the first letter of their name.

Learning Centers

Blocks (Alphabet Blocks)

Place stick-on letters from A to Z on square blocks, or photocopy the alphabet letter patterns (appendix p. 232) and tape them to the blocks. Encourage the children to arrange the blocks in alphabetical order. Try arranging the letters in sequences of four. Ask the children to identify the letter that is the same as the first letter of their name. *Can you find all the letters in your name?*

Fine Motor (My Favorite Letter)

Encourage the children to make their favorite alphabet letter out of playdough.

Language (ABC Train)

Photocopy the train patterns (appendix p. 236-237) to make an alphabet train. Make one engine and 26 cars. Print one letter on each train car (or use stick-on letters). Ask the children to arrange the cars in alphabetical order.

Writing (ABC Magnetic Letters)

Invite the children to arrange magnetic letters or the Alphabet Letter Patterns (appendix p. 232) in alphabetical order.

Outdoor Play or Music and Movement Activity

1. Play Alphabet Hopscotch. Use chalk to draw a grid with 13 rows and 2 columns on the sidewalk. Write one letter of the alphabet in each square, starting with "A" in the bottom left square and "B" in the bottom right square. Continue writing letters in order from left to right up the grid. Encourage the children to hop up the grid following the alphabetical sequence and saying each letter as they land on it.

2. Try some of these music and movement ideas:

    ♪ Invite the children to chant along with the "Alphabet Boogie" (*I Am Special* CD, Thomas Moore).

    ♪ Invite the children to dance with scarves to "A, You're Adorable" (*Musical Scarves & Activities* CD, Giorgiana Stewart, Kimbo).

    ♪ Encourage the children to sing along with songs on *A to Z, the Animals & Me* CD, Kimbo; "Nursery Rhyme Rap" (*Dr. Jean and Friends* CD, Jean Feldman); or "Alphabet Forward and Backwards" (*Keep on Singing and Dancing* CD, Jean Feldman).

REFLECTIONS

What is your favorite letter of the alphabet? Why?

Which letter is the first letter of the alphabet? Which letter is the last letter?

Annie Mae

Annie Mae
(Tune: Traditional)

Annie Mae, where are you going?
Up the stairs to take a bath.
Annie Mae with legs like toothpicks
And a neck like a giraffe.
Annie Mae stepped in the bathtub.
Annie Mae pulled out the plug.
Oh, my goodness!
Oh, my soul!
There goes Annie Mae down that hole.
Annie Mae? Annie Mae?
Gurgle, gurgle, glug.

Related Songs, Chants, and Rhymes

After My Bath

After my bath I try, try, try
To rub with a towel till I'm dry, dry, dry.
Hands to dry, and fingers and toes,
And two wet legs and a shiny nose.
Just think how much less time it'd take
If I were a dog and could shake, shake, shake!

Evan's Bath Song by Richele Bartkowiak (Tune: Rockabye, Baby)

Splishin' and a splashin'
In the bathtub.
When we take a bath
We clean and we scrub.
With a washcloth
And a little shampoo,
And when it's all over
We smell good as new.

Splishin' and a splashin'
That's what we do.
Don't forget Ducky.
He likes it, too.
Watchin' the bubbles
Dance in the tub.
Oh, how we love bath time
Rub-a-dub-dub!

THEME CONNECTIONS
Animals
Health
Humor
Parts of the Body
Self

There Was a Crooked Man

There was a crooked man who walked a crooked mile.
He found a crooked sixpence against a crooked stile.
He bought a crooked cat, which caught a crooked mouse.
And they all lived together in a crooked little house.

Literacy Activities

(Select one or two follow-up activities to do each time you sing a song or say a rhyme.)

Oral Language Development

1. Discuss new vocabulary words with the children, such as toothpick, giraffe, and gurgle.
2. Discuss phrases such as "Oh, my goodness!" and "Oh, my soul!" Explain that these expressions are called **exclamations** and are most often used to show emotion.

Phonological Awareness

1. Ask the children to identify the words in the song that sound like the sound they are trying to describe. Ask what the words "gurgle, gurgle, glug" are describing. Explain to the children that words that sound like the sound they are describing are called **onomatopoeia**.
2. Help the children identify the rhyming words in the song (for example, soul/hole, bath/giraffe, plug/glug). Sing "Michael Finnegan" on p. 35 or recite "There Was a Crooked Man" (see Related Songs, Chants, and Rhymes) for more rhyming words to explore.

Comprehension

1. Ask the children questions to determine what they understand about what happened in the song. *What happened to Annie Mae? How skinny would Annie Mae have to be in order to go down the drain?* You may want to demonstrate by using a potato chip can to represent a drain and inviting the children to see if they can put their hand inside the can. Make sure the edges of the can are smooth.
2. Ask the children questions to determine if they understand the **metaphors** used in the song. *If Annie Mae's legs are like toothpicks, what do they look like? If her neck is like a giraffe's neck, what does her neck look like?* Explain that these words in the song help us imagine (get a picture in our heads) what Annie Mae looks like. *What other ways could we describe someone's legs? What if we said, "Legs like an elephant"? What would those legs look like?*

3. If you sing "Michael Finnegan" (see p. 35) with the children, discuss nonsense words using "chinnegan" as an example. Why did the person who made up the song use "chinnegan?"

Learning Centers

Art (Annie Mae Portraits)

Encourage the children to draw a picture of Annie Mae or another funny character of their own design. Invite them to describe the character they have drawn. If they do not draw Annie Mae, encourage them to name their character.

Math (Giraffe Necks)

Give the children a 6' piece of yarn. Explain that the neck of a full-grown giraffe is about 6' long—the same length as the yarn. Encourage them to use the string to find something in the room that is the same length.

Science (Giraffes)

Provide pictures of giraffes and, if available, plastic giraffes. Encourage the children to describe a giraffe. *What color is the giraffe? What do the giraffe's legs look like? What does the giraffe's tail look like? Can you think of any other animals that look like giraffes?*

Water Play (Gurgle, Gurgle, Glug!)

Provide water and some water play items such as plastic bottles, turkey basters, eyedroppers, cups, strainers, and funnels. Challenge the children to find an item that will make a "gurgle, gurgle, glug" sound in the water.

Outdoor Play or Music and Movement Activity

1. Provide cardboard boxes to make tunnels in various sizes. Ask questions. *Which tunnels can you fit through? Which tunnels are too small to fit through?*
2. Sing along with "Annie Mae" (*Thinkable, Movable, Lovable Songs* CD, ProVideo Productions) or "Splish, Splash" (*Bean Bag Rock and Roll* CD, Kimbo).

BRAIN CONNECTION

Humor is good for the brain. When we laugh our bodies release endorphins, which act as memory fixatives. These endorphins also protect our immune system.

REFLECTIONS

Have you ever been worried about going down the drain in the bathtub? What have you learned today that helps you know there is no reason to worry?

What do you think Annie Mae's mother looks like? Why?

The Ants Go Marching

The Ants Go Marching
(Tune: Traditional)

The ants go marching one by one,
Hurrah, hurrah.
The ants go marching one by one,
Hurrah, hurrah.
The ants go marching one by one,
The little one stops to suck his thumb.
And they all go marching down
To the ground,
To get out
Of the rain.
BOOM! BOOM! BOOM! BOOM!

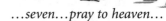

…two…tie her shoe…
…three…climb a tree…
…four…shut the door…
…five…take a dive…
…six…pick up sticks…

…seven…pray to heaven…
…eight…shut the gate…
…nine…check the time…
…ten…say "The End!"

THEME CONNECTIONS

Animals
Counting/Numbers
Humor
Insects
Science
Sound and
    Movement
Sounds of Language
Weather

Related Songs, Chants, and Rhymes

Anthill

Once I saw an anthill (make a fist with your hand)
With no ants about.
So I said, "Dear little ants,
Won't you please come out?"
Then, as if the little ants
Had heard my call,
One, two, three, four, five came out! (extend fingers one at a time)
And that was all.

The Insect Song (Tune: Head, Shoulders, Knees, and Toes)

Head, thorax, abdomen,
Abdomen.
Head, thorax, abdomen,
Abdomen.
Six legs, four wings, antennae too.
Head, thorax, abdomen,
Abdomen.

Little Ants by Pam Schiller (Tune: This Old Man)

Little ants marching by,
In a line that's mighty long,
With a hip, hop, happy, hi
Won't you join my song?
Little ants are marching on.

Little ants hopping high,
In a line that's mighty long,
With a hip, hop, happy, hi
Won't you join my song?
Little ants are hopping on.

Little ants sneaking by,
In a line that's mighty long,
With a hip, hop, happy, hi
Won't you join my song?
Little ants are sneaking on.

Little ants waving bye,
In a line that's mighty long,
With a hip, hop, happy, hi
Won't you join my song?
Little ants are waving bye.

SEE ALSO
"Little Ant's Hill"
    p. 140
"This Old Man"
    p. 198
"A Thunderstorm"
    p. 215

Literacy Activities

(Select one or two follow-up activities to do each time you sing a song or say a rhyme.)

Oral Language Development

1. Try substituting other verbs for "marching" or "hopping." Encourage the children to make suggestions. Have them clap out the syllables so that they understand that the words they substitute will need to have two syllables. Do they notice that "ing" is a consistent part of the action words they choose? The children may be better able to help with action words (**verbs**) after they sing "Little Ants" (above).

2. Ask the children where they think the ants might be going. Encourage imaginative answers. Make a list of the possibilities.

3. Encourage the children to describe their experiences with ants. *Has anyone seen a line of ants? Were the ants in a line or were they scattered?*

4. If possible, show photographs of ants. Use the photos to stimulate discussion of body parts, color, size, and so forth.

Phonological Awareness

1. Help the children identify the rhyming words in each verse (one/sun, two/shoe, and so on). Encourage them to think of other rhyming words.

2. Ask the children what the words "boom, boom, boom, boom" might be describing. *Is it the beat of a drum? Is it thunder? Why do you think that is what the words are describing?* Tell the children that "boom" can be an **onomatopoeia** word for both a drumbeat and for thunder. **Onomatopoeia** is a word that sounds like its meaning.

Learning Centers

Discovery (Drum Sounds)

Invite the children to play drums. Challenge them to create a marching cadence. *Do the drumbeats sound like thunder?* Ask them to try and make thunder sounds with their drums.

Games (Rhyming Word Match)

Write the rhyming words of "The Ants Go Marching" on index cards. Encourage the children to match the rhyming words. Ask questions while they are working. *Can you think of a word other than door that rhymes with four? What about five?*

Language (New Words That Rhyme)

Encourage the children to march like the ants in "The Ants Go Marching." Begin with one child and add a new child with each new verse of the song. Invite the children to think of new actions that will rhyme with the numbers. For example, one by one…to look at the sun, two by two…to say "boo-hoo," and so on.

Writing (Ants and Boom)

Write the words "ants" and "boom" on index cards. Provide magnetic letters and encourage the children to copy the words. Discuss the letters. Ask children to identify letters that are used more than once in the word "boom." Some children will be able to write the words. Suggest that they write the words on index cards and add them to their Word Box (shoebox collection of words they can write).

Outdoor Play or Music and Movement Activity

1. Encourage the children to act out "Little Ants" (see Related Songs, Chants, and Rhymes). Ask the children to help think of other ways the ants might travel. Point out that movement words like marching, spinning, and sneaking are called actions words (**verbs**).

2. Sing along with "The Ants Go Marching" (*Here Is Thumbkin!* CD, Kimbo).

REFLECTIONS
Where have you seen ants? Have you ever seen them walking in a line?

Tell me something you learned about ants today.

Apples and Bananas

Apples and Bananas
(Tune: Traditional)

I like to eat eat eat apples and bananas.
I like to eat eat eat apples and bananas.

I like to ate ate ate ay-puls and bay-nay-nays.
I like to ate ate ate ay-puls and bay-nay-nays.

I like eet eet eet ee-ples and bee-nee-nees.
I like eet eet eet ee-ples and bee-nee-nees.

I like to ite ite ite i-ples and by-ny-nys.
I like to ite ite ite i-ples and by-ny-nys.

I like to ote ote ote oh-pples and bo-no-nos.
I like to ote ote ote oh-pples and bo-no-nos.

I like to ute ute ute uu-pples and bu-nu-nus.
I like to ute ute ute uu-pples and bu-nu-nus.

Now we're through, through, through, through,
Now we're through with the apples and bananas,
Now we're through, through, through, through,
With A E I O and U.

THEME CONNECTIONS
Apples
Colors
Farms
Food
Friends
Growing Things
Nature
Shapes
Sun, Moon, Stars
Things That Go
    Together
Weather

Related Songs, Chants, and Rhymes

Apples and Bananas Chant
I want to eat,
I want to eat,
Eight apples and bananas.
I want to eat,
I want to eat,
Eight apples and bananas.
(Repeat, changing the vowel sound each time you recite the chant, just as with the song above.)

Johnny Appleseed (Tune: Traditional)

Oh, the earth is good to me,
And so I thank the earth,
For giving me the things I need:
The sun, the rain, and the apple seed.
The earth is good to me.

Little Red Apple

A little red apple grew high in a tree. (point up)
I looked up at it. (shade eyes and look up)
It looked down at me. (shade eyes and look down)
"Come down, please," I called. (use hand to motion downward)
And that little red apple fell right on my head. (tap the top of your head)

Oats, Peas, Beans, and Barley Grow (Tune: Traditional)

Oats, peas, beans, and barley grow.
Oats, peas, beans, and barley grow.
Neither you nor I nor anyone knows
How oats, peas, beans, and barley grow.
(supplemental illustration available)

Literacy Activities

(Select one or two follow-up activities to do each time you sing a song or say a rhyme.)

Oral Language Development

1. Discuss the children's experiences with fruits. *Which fruit do you like best? Where do you get fruit? Which fruits are red? Yellow? Orange? Can you eat the skin of a fruit?*

Phonological Awareness

1. Sing "Apples and Bananas," substituting "papayas" for "bananas". Ask the children which version they like best. *Has anyone ever eaten a papaya?*

Letter Knowledge and Recognition

1. Write "apples," "epples," "opples," and "upples" on index cards. Ask the children which letter is different in each word. *Does anyone know which word says "apple?"* If not, help them determine which word it is. Point out that apple begins with the letter "A."

Learning Centers

Language (Pick a Pair)

Cut out apples from red construction paper. Cut out pairs of rhyming word items from old workbooks or magazines. Glue them on the apple cutouts. Encourage the children to match the rhyming pairs of apples.

Math (Which Do You Like Best?)

Ask the children if they prefer apples or bananas. Give the children who prefer apples a red construction paper square to represent apples, and give those who prefer bananas a yellow construction paper square to represent bananas. Ask them to line up their squares on the floor in a one-to-one correspondence. *Do more children like apples or bananas?*

Snack (Apples and Bananas)

Provide apple slices, banana slices, and skewers. Encourage the children to make apple and banana kabobs. As they work on constructing their snack, ask them to describe each fruit. *Which fruit is easier to push onto the stick? Why?*

Writing (Apples and Bananas)

Provide word cards with either the word "apples" or "bananas" written on them. Encourage the children to use magnetic letters or chalk to copy the words. Ask them which word appears to have the most letters. Demonstrate how to match the letters in the words in one-to-one correspondence to check their choice. *Do any letters show up in both words?*

Some children will be able to write the words. Suggest that they write the words on index cards and add them to their Word Box (shoebox collection of words they can write).

Outdoor Play or Music and Movement Activity

1. Play Fruit Salad. Divide the children into four groups and seat each group in a corner of an imaginary square. Label the groups bananas, apples, oranges, and grapes. Give each group construction paper squares or colored scarves (red for apples, yellow for bananas, orange for oranges, and purple for grapes). Select a child to be IT. IT stands in the center, closes his or her eyes, and says, "Fruit basket turn over." The children drop their squares, run to another group area, and pick up a new square. They must find a square in order to stay in the new group. IT tries to catch a child before he or she is able to pick up a new square. If successful, he or she becomes part of the group and the caught child becomes IT. If not successful, he or she continues the game as IT.
2. Sing along with "Apples and Bananas" (*Where Is Thumbkin?* CD, Kimbo).

BRAIN CONNECTIONS

Both apples and bananas are good "brain foods." The brain operates well on foods that supply complex carbohydrates such as fruits, but has a difficult time operating on foods that are primarily simple carbohydrates, such as cookies, candies, and syrups. Simple carbohydrates make thinking sluggish!

REFLECTIONS

Which fruit do you like best? Apples or bananas? Why?

How are apples and bananas alike? How are they different?

Are You Sleeping?

Are You Sleeping?
(Tune: Traditional)

Are you sleeping,
Are you sleeping,
Brother John, Brother John?
Morning bells are ringing,
Morning bells are ringing.
Ding! Dong! Ding!
Ding! Dong! Ding!

Related Songs, Chants, and Rhymes

Jingle Bells (Tune: Traditional)

Jingle bells, jingle bells,
Jingle all the way!
Oh, what fun it is to ride
In a one-horse open sleigh!
Hey!
Jingle bells, jingle bells,
Jingle all the way!
Oh, what fun it is to ride
In a one-horse open sleigh!

Lazy Mary (Tune: Mulberry Bush)

Lazy Mary, will you get up,
Will you get up, will you get up?
Lazy Mary, will you get up
This cold and frosty morning?

THEME CONNECTIONS

Animals
Families
Holidays/Celebrations
Languages
Naptime/Sleeping
Sound and
    Movement
Time of Day
Travel/Transportation
Weather

No, no, Mother, I won't get up,
I won't get up, I won't get up.
No, no, Mother, I won't get up,
This cold and frosty morning.

Literacy Activities

(Select one or two follow-up activities to do each time you sing a song or say a rhyme.)

Phonological Awareness

1. Discuss the sound the bells make in the song—"ding, dong, ding." *Do the words sound like the sound they are describing? What other sounds do bells make?*

2. Write "ding, dong, ding" on a chalkboard or chart paper. Read the words, placing your hand under each word as you say it. Read the words a second time emphasizing the first letter sound, and at the same time, drawing a line under the first letter of each word. Point out that the letters are all the same and that they all make the same sound. Tell the children that when several words in a row have the same beginning letter and sound it is called **alliteration**.

Letter Knowledge and Recognition

1. Write the words "ding" and "dong" on index cards. Read the cards to the children. Encourage them to look at the cards side by side and point out which letters are the same in each word and which letter is different. Save the cards for the writing center.

Learning Centers

Discovery (Bell Bags)

Place one jingle bell in an envelope and seal it. Place two bells in a second envelope and seal it. Continue with three, four, and five bells. Ask the children to arrange the sealed envelopes in order, from softest to the loudest sound. *Is there another way the envelopes can be arranged in the same order without ringing the bells?* (weight of the envelopes)

Dramatic Play (Sleepy Time)

Place sleep props such as pillows, blankets, an alarm clock, lullaby music, and a stuffed animal in the Dramatic Play center. Encourage the children to pretend that they are going to sleep at night. Ask about their bedtime routines.

SEE ALSO
"Hush, Little Baby"
p. 107
"Rockabye, Baby"
p. 107
"Ten in the Bed"
p. 186

Math (Sleepy Eyes and Wakeful Eyes)

Give the children ten large wiggle eyes. Ask them to hold the eyes in their hands and then drop them on a tray or a plate. Eyes that land face up are "wakeful" eyes. Eyes that land face down are "sleepy" eyes. Encourage the children to match the eyes one to one to see if they have more sleepy eyes or more wakeful eyes. Ask questions. *Is it possible to have the same number of each? Is it possible for all the eyes to be sleepy or for all the eyes to be wakeful?*

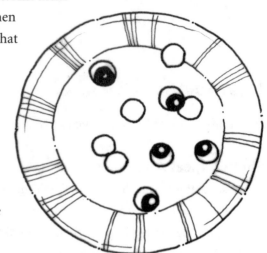

Writing (Ding and Dong)

Provide the index cards with "ding" and "dong" written on them. Invite the children to copy the words with magnetic letters. Ask how they can change the words back and forth by moving only one letter. Some children will be able to write the words. Suggest that they write the words on index cards and add them to their Word Box (shoebox collection of words they can write).

Outdoor Play or Music and Movement Activity

1. Play Ding, Ding, Dong as you would Duck, Duck, Goose. Sit children in a circle. Select a child to be IT. IT walks around the outside of the circle, tapping each player on the head and saying, "Ding." Eventually IT taps a player and says "Dong" instead. The tapped player gets up and chases IT around the circle. If she taps IT before he gets around the circle, she gets to go back to her place. If she doesn't, she becomes the new IT and the game continues.
2. Sing along with "Frère Jacques" (*Walt Disney Records: Children's Favorite Songs Vol. 2* CD), "Are You Sleeping?" (*Here Is Thumbkin!* CD, Kimbo), or "Rise and Shine" (*A Whole Lot of Animals* CD by Joel Reese).

BRAIN CONNECTIONS

Sleep is an important part of proper brain function. During sleep the brain is able to do some "housekeeping" that allows it to be ready to take in more information when we awaken.

REFLECTIONS

How do you wake up in the morning?

Have you ever woken up to an alarm clock?

How do you like to be woken up in the morning?

Baby Bumblebee

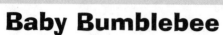

Baby Bumblebee
adapted by Richele Bartkowiak (Tune: Baby Bumblebee)

I caught myself a baby bumblebee.
Won't my mommy be so proud of me?
I caught myself a baby bumblebee
Ouch! He stung me!

I'm talking to my baby bumblebee.
Won't my mommy be so proud of me?
I'm talking to my baby bumblebee,
"Oh," he said, "I'm sorry."

I'm letting go my baby bumblebee.
Won't my mommy be so proud of me?
I'm letting go my baby bumblebee,
Look he's happy to be free!

Related Songs, Chants, and Rhymes

Baby Bumblebee (Tune: Traditional)

I caught myself a baby bumblebee.
Won't my mommy be so proud of me?
I caught myself a baby bumblebee,
Ouch! He stung me!

I'm squishing up my baby bumblebee.
Won't my mommy be so proud of me?
I'm squishing up my baby bumblebee,
"Oh! It's yucky!"

I'm wiping off my baby bumblebee.
Won't my mommy be so proud of me?
I'm wiping off the baby bumblebee,
Now my mommy won't be mad at me.

**THEME
CONNECTIONS**
Animals
Caring for Our
    World
Families
Insects

SEE ALSO
"Fiddle Dee Dee"
    p. 51
"Frog Went A-
    Courtin'" p. 70
"Little Bee's Hive"
    p. 140

Hickey Picky Bumblebee

Hickey picky bumblebee
Won't you say your name to me? (direct the question to a child by pointing to her)
(child says name, e.g., Gabrielle)
Gabrielle!
Let's clap it—Ga-bri-elle. (clap each syllable)
Let's snap it—Ga-bri-elle. (snap each syllable)
Let's tap it—Ga-bri-elle. (tap foot to the syllables)

Continue repeating the verse and pointing to different children.

Literacy Activities

(Select one or two follow-up activities to do each time you sing a song or say a rhyme.)

Comprehension

1. Sing the original version of the song (see Related Songs, Chants, and Rhymes). Ask a child to describe what happens in the song. Why did the child smash the bee? You may want to use this opportunity to warn children to stay away from bees.
2. Sing the adapted version of the song. *How is it different? Why did the child let the bumblebee go free? Which version of the song do you like best? Why?*
3. Show the children photographs of bees. Encourage the children to discuss when and where they have seen bees. *Where were the bees? What were the bees doing? Has anyone ever been stung? What did it feel like to be stung?*

Listening (segmentation)

1. Say the word "bumblebee," emphasizing the syllables (bum-ble-bee). Invite the children to clap out the syllables. This is called **segmentation**. Ask them to count the syllables as they clap. Then ask them to clap the syllables in their names. (If this is the first time you have done this type of activity, you will have to help each child with his or her name.) *Does anyone have a name with three syllables?* Have the children clap the syllables in "baby bumblebee." *Now how many syllables do you hear?* Count them together.
2. Recite the segmentation chant, "Hickey Picky Bumblebee" (see above) with the children.

Phonological Awareness

1. Help the children identify the rhyming words in the song (bee/me, bee/free).
2. Write the words "baby bumblebee" on a chalkboard or chart paper. Point out the /b/ sound in baby bumblebee. Say the words, emphasizing the beginning sounds as you underline the first letters (b). Explain that when several words in a row have the same beginning sounds, it is called **alliteration**. Teach the children the following tongue twister:
    Bessie bumblebee believes bees are the best buzzers.

Letter Knowledge and Recognition

1. Write the words "baby bumblebee" on a chalkboard or chart paper. Write the letter "b" on the bottom of the chart paper. Invite a volunteer to point to the letter "b's" in "baby bumblebee." *How many "b's" are there?* Underline the letter "b" in each word as you count them.

Learning Centers

Dramatic Play (Beezy Bee Puppets)

Encourage children to draw and color bees, cut them out, and then glue them to craft sticks to make puppets. Encourage them to re-enact the story using their bee puppets.

Science (Bee Search)

Take the children on a nature walk in search of bees. *Where do you look for bees? What should you do if you see bees?* Discuss bee safety.

Snack (Bread and Honey)

Serve the children bread and honey for snack. Discuss the honey. *How does it taste? Is it thick or thin? Can anyone describe the color of honey? Can you think of something else that is the same color? Where does honey come from?*

Writing (I Can Spell "Bee")

Provide an index card with the word "bee" written on it. Encourage the children to copy the word using magnetic letters. *Which letter is used two times?* Some children will be able to write the word. Suggest that they write the word on an index card and add it to their Word Box (shoebox collection of words they can write).

Outdoor Play or Music and Movement Activity

1. Bees do a "waggle dance" to help other bees locate honey. They wiggle the tail sections of their bodies and fly in a circle that moves toward the source of the honey. Teach the children how to do a waggle dance. Place a flower or something to represent a flower in the center of the room. Put on some "bee buzzing" music and encourage them to "waggle dance" around the flower. Move the flower from time to time to create a new pattern.

2. Sing along with "Baby Bumblebee" (*Thinkable, Movable, Lovable Songs* CD, ProVideo Productions) or the traditional version of "Baby Bumblebee" (*Here Is Thumbkin!* CD, Kimbo).

REFLECTIONS

What did you learn about bees today?

How are bees like flies? How are they different? What other insect stings?

Bingo

Bingo
(Tune: Traditional)

There was a farmer had a dog,
And Bingo was his name-o.
B-I-N-G-O!
B-I-N-G-O!
B-I-N-G-O!
And Bingo was his name-o!

There was a farmer had a dog,
And Bingo was his name-o.
(Clap)-I-N-G-O!
(Clap)-I-N-G-O!
(Clap)-I-N-G-O!
And Bingo was his name-o!

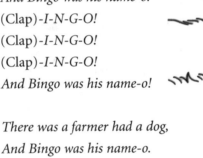

There was a farmer had a dog,
And Bingo was his name-o.
(Clap, clap)-N-G-O!
(Clap, clap)-N-G-O!
(Clap, clap)-N-G-O!
And Bingo was his name-o!

(Continue singing, substituting a
clap for the next letter each
time until there are no letters left.)

**THEME
CONNECTIONS**
Animals
Farms
Food
Humor
Languages
Occupations
Pets

Related Songs, Chants, and Rhymes

Fido (Tune: Reuben, Reuben)

I had a little dog
And his name was Fido.
He was nothing but a pup.
He could stand up on his hind legs
If you held his front legs up.

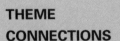

My Dog Rags (Tune: Six White Ducks)

I have a dog and his name is Rags, (point to self)

He eats so much that his tummy sags, (put hands together in front of stomach)

His ears flip flop and his tail wig wags, (bend first left and then right hand at wrist)

And when he walks he zig, zig, zags! (make an imaginary "Z" with index finger)

Flip, flop, wig, wag, zig, zags! (bend each wrist, wiggle hips, make "z")

Old Mother Hubbard

Old Mother Hubbard

Went to the cupboard

To give her poor dog a bone.

When she got there

The cupboard was bare,

And so the poor dog had none.

Literacy Activities

(Select one or two follow-up activities to do each time you sing a song or say a rhyme.)

Listening

1. Suggest that the children clap loudly as they spell "Bingo," and then clap softly as they spell it. Encourage them to sing loudly when they clap loudly and sing softly when they clap softly. *How does the song change with the volume of clapping and singing?* Clapping loudly and softly is easier, and perhaps more meaningful, for children than clapping the missing letters.

Phonological Awareness

1. Point out that in the song, the word "name" is changed by adding the letter "o" to it. *How is it different? Why does the song use "name-o" instead of "name?" What word does "name-o" rhyme with? How would the song be different if the dog's name was Sadie?*

Letter Knowledge and Recognition

1. Write the letters "B", "I", "N", "G", and "O" on separate index cards. Have volunteers hold up the appropriate letter as it is mentioned in the song.

SEE ALSO

"Hop and Rags" p. 101

"Where, Oh, Where, Has My Little Dog Gone?" p. 102

"Whose Dog Are Thou?" p. 102

Learning Centers

Blocks (Farm Life)

Provide props (such as plastic animals, tractors, silos, and so on) for the children to build a farm. Make sure to include a dog with the animals. Talk with the children as they build. Ask them to name animals. *Why don't we see elephants and giraffes on farms?*

Gross Motor (Feed the Dog)

Give the children a dog bowl and a beanbag with a paper bone attached. Encourage them to toss the bone (beanbag) into the bowl.

Language (Bingo Name Puzzles)

Make Bingo Name Puzzles. Write "Bingo" on two or three pieces of 4" x 12" tagboard, leaving enough space between the letters to cut them apart into puzzle pieces. Encourage the children to put the puzzles together. What strategies do they use to put the puzzles together? If they recognize the letters, they may actually spell the name as a means of connecting the pieces.

Writing (I Can Spell Bingo)

Give the children a set of index cards with each letter of Bingo's name written on each card. Also provide blank index cards. Encourage them to make their own set of letter cards. When they are finished, help them place the cards in the correct order to spell "Bingo."

Outdoor Play or Music and Movement Activity

1. Sing along with "Bingo" (*Walt Disney Records: Children's Favorite Songs Vol. 2* CD), "BINGO" (*Twinkle, Twinkle, Jazzy Star* CD, Thomas Moore), "Rags" (*Thinkable, Movable, Lovable Songs* CD, ProVideo Production), or "Oh, Where, Oh, Where Has My Little Dog Gone?" (*Walt Disney Records: Children's Favorite Songs Vol. 4* CD).

REFLECTIONS

Why do farms make good homes for dogs?

What is the best thing about having a dog for a pet?

34

Catalina Magnalina

Catalina Magnalina
(Tune: Traditional)

She had a peculiar name but she wasn't to blame.
She got it from her mother, who's the same, same, same.

Chorus
Catalina Magnalina, Hootensteiner Bogentwiner
Hogan Logan Bogan was her name.
She had two peculiar teeth in her mouth,
One pointed north and the other pointed south.

Chorus

She had two peculiar eyes in her head,
One was purple and the other was red.

Chorus

She had two peculiar hairs on her chin,
One stuck out and the other stuck in.

Chorus

Related Songs, Chants, and Rhymes

Michael Finnegan (Tune: Traditional)

There was an old man named Michael Finnegan.
He had whiskers on his chinnegan.
They fell out and then grew in again.
Poor old Michael Finnegan,
Begin again.

There was an old man named Michael Finnegan.
He went fishing with a pin again.
Caught a fish and dropped it in again.
Poor old Michael Finnegan,
Begin again.

THEME CONNECTIONS

Animals
Colors
Families
Humor
Opposites
Parts of the Body

SEE ALSO
"Annie Mae" p. 17
"Miss Mary Mack"
p. 143

There was an old man named Michael Finnegan.
He grew fat and then grew thin again.
Then he died and had to begin again.
Poor old Michael Finnegan,
Begin again.

Risseldy, Rosseldy (Tune: Traditional)
I married my wife in the month of June,
Risseldy, rosseldy, mow, mow, mow,
I carried her off in a silver spoon,
Rosseldy, rosseldy, hey bambassity,
Nickety, nackety, retrical quality,
Willowby, wallowby, mow, mow, mow.

She combed her hair but once a year,
Risseldy, rosseldy, mow, mow, mow,
With every rake she shed a tear,
Rosseldy, rosseldy, hey bambassity,
Nickety, nackety, retrical quality,
Willowby, wallowby, mow, mow, mow.

She churned her butter in her Dad's old boot,
Risseldy, rosseldy, mow, mow, mow.
And for a dasher used her foot,
Rosseldy, rosseldy, hey bambassity,
Nickety, nackety, retrical quality,
Willowby, wallowby, mow, mow, mow.

Literacy Activities

(Select one or two follow-up activities to do each time you sing a song or say a rhyme.)

Listening (Segmentation)

1. Encourage the children to clap the syllables for the word "Catalina." Ask them to clap the syllables in their own names. (If this is the first time you have done this activity, you will need to help each child with his or her name.) *Does anyone have four syllables in their name like Catalina does?* Challenge them to clap the syllables for Catalina's whole name. That's a lot of claps!

Oral Language Development

1. Discuss the opposites mentioned in the song (in/out and north/south). Sing "Michael Finnegan" (see Related Songs, Chants, and Rhymes) and talk about the opposites mentioned in it (out/in, caught/dropped, and fat/thin).

Phonological Awareness

1. Invite the children to find the rhyming words in the song (name/same, head/red, chin/in, mouth/south). *What about the rhyming words in Catalina's name?*

2. Invite the children to create a rhyming word to go with their own name.

Letter Knowledge and Recognition

1. Use magnetic letters to write the names "Hogan," "Logan," and "Bogan" on a magnetic board or a cookie sheet. Ask the children to identify the letters in each name that are alike and the letters in each name that are different. Remove the first letter in each name. Ask if any letters are different now. Place the "H" back in front of the first set of letters. Read it. Remove the "H" and place the "L" in its place. Read the name. Remove the "L" and replace it with the "B." Read the name. Are the children able to see that the first letter changes the sound of the name?

Learning Centers

Art (Catalina Portraits)

Challenge the children to draw a picture of Catalina Magnalina. Encourage them to come up with their own funny features to add.

Fine Motor (Name Puzzles)

Make Name Puzzles. Write each child's name on a strip of 4" x 12" tagboard. Leave enough space between the letters to cut them apart into puzzle pieces. Encourage the children to put the puzzles together.

Science (Up Close Eyes)

Provide a magnifying glass and encourage the children to look closely at each other's eyes. *What color are the eyes? Does anyone have one eye that is one color and the other eye that is another color?*

If available, invite children to explore a compass. Help them find north and south.

Writing (Hogan, Logan, Bogan)

Encourage the children to practice writing "Hogan," "Logan," and "Bogan" with the magnetic letters. Show them how moving one letter makes the words interchangeable.

Outdoor Play or Music and Movement Activity

1. Play Catalina Says as you would Simon Says. Choose one child to be "Catalina." All the other children stand side-by-side in a line facing Catalina. The child playing Catalina gives the other children orders that they have to carry out, but only when the orders follow the phrase "Catalina says..." (e.g., "Catalina says touch your nose"). If a child follows an order that Catalina did not say (e.g., "Touch your nose"), then he is out and must sit down. The last child standing becomes the new Catalina for the next game of "Catalina Says."

2. Sing along with "Katalina Matalina" (*Dr. Jean Sings Silly Songs*, Jean Feldman) or "Michael Finnegan" (*Where Is Thumbkin?* CD, Kimbo).

BRAIN CONNECTIONS

Humor is good for you. It causes endorphins to be released into your bloodstream that help boost your immune system and your ability to remember.

REFLECTIONS

Do you have any friends who do silly things? What kind of things do they do?

Does anyone in your family have a long name? What is that person's name?

Hogan

Logan

Bogan

Chocolate Rhyme

Chocolate Rhyme

One, two, three, cho— (count with fingers)
One, two, three, co—
One, two, three, la—
One, two, three, te!
Stir, stir the chocolate. (make stirring motion)

Related Songs, Chants, and Rhymes

The Ice Cream Chant

I scream.
You scream.
We all scream for ice cream!

One Potato, Two Potato

One potato, two potato, (make two fists, alternate tapping one on top of the other)
Three potato, four,
Five potato, six potato,
Seven potato, more.
Eight potato, nine potato,
Where is ten?
Now we must count over again.

Peas Porridge Hot

Peas porridge hot (make up a partner clap)
Peas porridge cold,
Peas porridge in the pot
Nine days old.
Some like it hot.
Some like it cold.
Some like in the pot
Nine days old!

THEME CONNECTIONS
Counting/Numbers
Food
Seasons

Rima de Chocolate (Chocolate Rhyme in Spanish)

Uno, dos, tres, cho—
Uno, dos, tres, co—
Uno, dos, tres, la—
Uno, dos, tres, te!
Bate, bate, chocolate.

Literacy Activities

(Select one or two follow-up activities to do each time you sing a song or say a rhyme.)

Listening (Segmentation)

1. Clap out the syllables in the word "chocolate." *How many syllables are there?* Ask the children if any of them have a name with three syllables. Pronounce chocolate as it is broken apart in the chant: cho-co-la-te. *Now how many syllables do you hear?* Explain that this rhyme was originally written in Spanish and that in Spanish, the word is pronounced "cho-co-la-te" (with a long "o" in both places).

Oral Language Development

1. Encourage the children to tell you how they think hot chocolate is made. Accept all methods of preparation. Ask the children what they like to eat with their hot chocolate.

Print Awareness

1. Write the chant on chart paper or on the chalkboard. Place your hand under the words as you read them to the children. Recite the chant a couple of times. Discuss how print progresses from the left to right and top to bottom. *Which letter does "chocolate" begin with?*

Learning Centers

Dramatic Play (Hot Chocolate for Sale)

Provide props such as cups, empty soda bottles, napkins, cash register, play money, aprons, and signs. Encourage the children to create a Beverage Stand. Discuss the location of their stand and the items on their menu. Help them create menus and a marque. Ask them questions. *What beverages do you sell? How much does a cup of hot chocolate cost? Do you sell anything other than beverages? Have you seen beverage stands before? Where?*

Language (1, 2, 3)

Copy the cards below and on the next page. Encourage the children to match the correct numeral to the number word. Place the appropriate number of dots on the back of each set of cards so that the children can check their own work.

one

two

three

1

2

3

Snack (Hot Chocolate)

Encourage the children to follow the Hot Chocolate Rebus directions (appendix p. 230) for making a cup of hot chocolate. Ask questions as the children prepare their chocolate. *Is the recipe similar to the way you thought a cup of hot chocolate is made? Which part of the procedure is like what you thought? Which part is different?*

Writing (I Can Write "Chocolate")

Write the word "chocolate" on a sheet of paper and encourage the children to copy it with magnetic letters. *Which letters are in the word "chocolate" twice?* Some children will be able to write the word. Suggest that they write "chocolate" on an index card and add it to their Word Box (shoebox collection of words they can write).

Outdoor Play or Music and Movement Activity

1. Play Cooperative Musical Marshmallows as you would Cooperative Musical Chairs. This game is a variation of Musical Chairs. Puff up a white sheet to look like a marshmallow and place it in the middle of the floor. Play a piece of music. Encourage the children to walk around the circle until the music stops. When the music stops everyone steps onto the marshmallow (sheet). The idea is to get everyone on so everyone wins. Repeat for more fun.

2. Try some of these music and movement ideas:
   - Encourage the children to sing along with "Make Myself Some Cookies" or "Corn on the Cob" (*I Am Special* CD, Thomas Moore). Invite the children to describe what they like to eat with their corn on the cob.
   - Invite the children to sing along with "Vegetable Song" (*Thomas Moore Sings the Family* CD, Thomas Moore).

REFLECTIONS

Can you make hot chocolate? How would you make it?

Would a cup of hot chocolate taste better in the winter or the summer? Why? What kind of chocolate drink might be good in the summer? Why?

The Color Song

The Color Song
**(Tune: "Dinah, won't you blow?" verse of
I've Been Workin' on the Railroad)**

Red is the color for an apple to eat.
Red is the color for cherries, too.
Red is the color for strawberries.
I like red, don't you?

Blue is the color for the summer sky.
Blue is the color for baby things, too.
Blue is the color of my sister's eyes.
I like blue, don't you?

Yellow is the color for the great big sun.
Yellow is the color for lemonade, too.
Yellow is the color of a baby chick.
I like yellow, don't you?

Orange is the color for the oranges.
Orange is the color for carrots, too.
Orange is the color of a jack-o-lantern.
I like orange, don't you?

Green is the color for the leaves on the trees.
Green is the color for green peas, too.
Green is the color of a watermelon.
I like green, don't you?

Purple is the color for a bunch of grapes.
Purple is the color for grape juice, too.
Purple is the color of Harold's crayon,
I like purple, don't you?

Related Songs, Chants, and Rhymes

Color Chants by Pam Schiller
I Like Blue

I like blue,
I really, really do.
I like blue,
Do you like it, too?
I like white clouds on blue skies,
I like large ships on blue oceans,

I like the blue color of my sister's eyes
I like blue lotions and notions.
I like blue,
I really, really do.
I like blue,
Do you like it, too?

**THEME
CONNECTIONS**
Colors
Things I Like/
   Favorite Things

SEE ALSO
"Great Green Gobs"
p. 89
"The Green Grass
Grew All
Around" p. 87
"The Iguana in
Lavender
Socks" p. 127

I Like Yellow

I like yellow, yellow is swell.
I like yellow - bet you can tell.
Yellow kittens, yellow beach balls,
Yellow mittens, bright yellow walls.
Yellow flowers, sweet yellow bees
Big yellow leaves in yellow trees.
Yellow, yellow, yellow, yellow,
I'm a happy yellow fellow!

I Like Red

I like red.
I like it a bunch.
I like red jam. I like red punch.
I like red flowers.
I like red shoes.
Red is the color I always choose.
I like red hair.
Oh, can't you see?
Red is the only color for me.

I Like Green

I like green.
I like it a lot.
I like green frogs,
Believe it or not.
Green ribbons are keen.
Green clover is neat.
I really love green.
It can't be beat.
I like green fish.
Oh, can't you see?
Think what you wish.
Green's the color for me.

Literacy Activities

(Select one or two follow-up activities to do each time you sing a song or say a rhyme.)

Oral Language Development

1. Encourage the children to name things that are the color red. Then ask them to name things that are blue, yellow, and green. Encourage each child to name his or her favorite color. Ask them why they like that color.
2. Sing "If You're Happy and You Know It." Instead of clapping your hands, stomping your feet, or shouting "hooray," have the children point to something red, something yellow, then blue, and finally green.

Letter Knowledge and Recognition

1. Use corresponding color markers to write the color words "red," "yellow," "blue," and "green" on index cards. Ask the children to read the words. *How do you know what the word says?* Tell them that someday they will be able to read the words because they will learn to recognize combinations of letters just like they recognize colors.
2. Show each card separately and let the children identify the letters that they recognize.

Learning Centers

Fine Motor (Red Plus Blue Equals)

Give each child a small ball of red playdough and a small ball of blue playdough. Encourage them to mix the two balls together. *What happens? Can you make the new color darker? Lighter? How?*

Language (Color Books)

Make a plastic bag book for each child. Staple five resealable plastic bags together along the bottom of the bags. Place a sheet of tagboard inside each bag with a color word written on it. Use the color ink that corresponds to the word. The children cut pictures from magazines for each color and place them in their books.

Science (Colored Lights)

Provide several pieces of irregularly cut pieces of colored acetate or cellophane and a light source such as an overhead projector or flashlight. Encourage the children to explore the colors created on a blank wall by projecting the light through the colored sheets. *What happens when you mix two colors by overlapping them? Can you arrange the sheets to make a design?*

Writing (Color Words)

Give the children index cards with color words written on them in the color that corresponds to the word. Provide tracing paper and crayons. Encourage the children to trace the letters using the color crayon that corresponds to the color word they are tracing.

Some children will be able to write the words. Suggest that they write the words on index cards and add them to their Word Box (shoebox collection of words they can write).

Outdoor Play or Music and Movement Activity

1. On a sunny day, give each child a large sheet of colored cellophane. Demonstrate how to hold the sheet over their heads to create colored shadows on the ground. Show them how to put to colors together to create a third color.
2. Sing along with "Color Song" (*Where Is Thumbkin?* CD, Kimbo) or "At the Easel" (*I Am Special* CD, Thomas Moore).

BRAIN CONNECTION

Colors impact our brain functions. Bright colors, such as reds, yellows, and oranges increase alertness. Blues, greens, and purples create a calming effect. Pale yellow is the optimum color for learning. Red stimulates appetite.

REFLECTIONS

How does the color red make you feel? What about the color blue? Share the brain research connection (see above) with the children.

What do you think it means when people say "I feel blue?"

Do You Know The Muffin Man?

Do You Know the Muffin Man?

(Tune: Traditional)

Oh, do you know the muffin man,
The muffin man, the muffin man?
Oh, do you know the muffin man
Who lives on Drury Lane?

Oh, yes I know the muffin man,
The muffin man, the muffin man.
Oh, yes I know the muffin man
Who lives on Drury Lane.

Related Songs, Chants, and Rhymes

The Donut Song (Tune: Turkey in the Straw)

Oh, I ran around the corner,
And I ran around the block.
I ran right in to the baker shop.
I grabbed me a donut,
Right out of the grease,
And I handed the lady,
A five-cent piece.
She looked at the nickel,
And she looked at me.
She said, "This nickel
Ain't no good to me.
There's a hole in the nickel
And it goes right through."
Said I, "There's a hole in your donut, too!
Thanks for the donut. Good-bye!" (spoken)

THEME CONNECTIONS

Babies
Community
Workers
Cooking
Counting/Numbers
Families
Food
Humor
Money
Neighborhoods
Occupations

Hot Cross Buns!

Hot cross buns! Hot cross buns!
One a penny, two a penny,
Hot cross buns!
If your daughters do not like them
Give them to your sons.

But if you haven't any
Of these pretty elves,
You cannot do better
Than eat them yourselves.

SEE ALSO
"Nursery Rhyme
Rap" p. 14

Pat-a-Cake

Pat-a-cake, pat-a-cake, baker's man. (clap hands together)
Bake me a cake as fast as you can.
Roll it, (roll hands over each other)
And pat it, (pat hands together)
And mark it with B, (draw B in the air)
And put it in the oven for baby and me. (touch tummy)

Who Stole the Cookies From the Cookie Jar?

(A group of children forms a circle. Decide who will be called first.)
Group: *Who stole the cookies from the cookie jar?*
(Child) *took the cookies from the cookie jar.*
Child: *Who, me?*
Group: *Yes, you!*
Child: *Couldn't be.*
Group: *Then who?*
Child: (Different child, chosen by first child) *took the cookie from the cookie jar.*
New child: *Who, me?*
Group: *Yes, you!*
New child: *Couldn't be.*
Group: *Then who?*

Pat your thighs and snap in a rhythmic motion as you say the chant. Continue until everyone has been accused. End with accusing the cookie monster.

Literacy Activities

(Select one or two follow-up activities to do each time you sing a song or say a rhyme.)

Oral Language Development

1. Ask the children what they think a muffin man is. *What does he sell? Is there another name for a person who sells baked goods? What is it?*
2. Ask the children what kind of muffins they like. Make a list of all the different kinds of muffins they mention. If the children don't mention many types, add some to the list and describe their flavors to the children.

Phonological Awareness

1. Write the tongue twister below on chart paper. Underline the first letters of each word that begins with the letter "M." Ask the children to identify the letter. Remind them that when consecutive words begin with the same letter sound it is called **alliteration**. Encourage the children to "read" the tongue twister with you three times quickly.

The muffin man makes multigrain muffins on Monday.

Letter Knowledge and Recognition

1. Write "muffin man" on chart paper. Ask the children to identify the first letter in each word. *Which letters appear more than once in the two words?*

Learning Centers

Games (Who Took the Cookie?)

Play "Who Stole the Cookies From the Cookie Jar?" (See Related Songs, Chants, and Rhymes). Substitute "muffin" for "cookie" and "muffin tin" for "cookie jar."

Language (Where Do You Live?)

Invite the children to tell you the name of their street. Write the street name (and/or full address) on drawing paper. Let the children draw pictures of their homes.

Math (Muffin Snacks)

Provide a variety of small muffins for snack. Ask the children to mark a graph showing which muffin type is their favorite.

Writing (Bakery Signs)

Provide markers, crayons, paper, and a list of possible bakery signs. Encourage the children to create additional signs for the bakery.

Outdoor Play or Music and Movement Activity

1. Take the children into a classroom of toddlers and invite them to teach the little ones to do Pat-a-Cake.
2. Play "Rock-n-Roll Pat-a-Cake" (*Songs for the Whole Day* CD, Thomas Moore). Invite the children to pat-a-cake and sing along, or invite them to sing along to "The Muffin Man" (*Songs Children Love to Sing* CD, Thomas Moore).

REFLECTIONS
Which kind of muffin is your favorite? Why?

How are muffins and cookies alike? How are they different?

Do Your Ears Hang Low?

Do Your Ears Hang Low?
(Tune: Turkey in the Straw)

Do your ears hang low? (point to your ears)

Do they wobble to and fro? (move your hands side to side)

Can you tie them in a knot? (make a tying motion)

Can you tie them in a bow? (pretend to tie a bow)

Can you throw them o'er your shoulder, (toss your clasped hands over shoulder)

Like a Continental soldier? (salute)

Do your ears hang low? (point to your ears)

Do your ears hang high?

Do they reach up to the sky?

Do they wrinkle when they're wet?

Do they straighten when they're dry?

Can you wave them at your neighbor,

With an element of flavor?

Do your ears hang high?

Do your ears hang wide?

Do they flap from side to side?

Do they wave in the breeze,

From the slightest little sneeze?

Can you soar above the nation,

With a feeling of elation?

Do your ears hang wide?

**THEME
CONNECTIONS**
Humor
Parts of the Body
Spatial
    Relationships

SEE ALSO
"The Grand Old
    Duke of York"
    p. 81
"Humpty Dumpty's
    New Ears"
    p. 104
"Yankee Doodle"
    p. 81

Related Songs, Chants, and Rhymes

Where Do You Wear Your Ears?

Where do you wear your ears?

Underneath your hat?

Where do you wear your ears?

Yes ma'am, just like that.

Where do you wear your ears?

Say where, you sweet, sweet child.

Where do you wear your ears?

On both ends of my smile!

Literacy Activities

(Select one or two follow-up activities to do each time you sing a song or say a rhyme.)

Oral Language Development

1. Show the children photos of animals with long ears such as donkeys, rabbits, elephants, and cocker spaniels. Use the photos to stimulate discussion about long ears.
2. Discuss words that may be new vocabulary, such as "to and fro," "wobble," "continental," "knot," and "bow."

Phonological Awareness

1. Help the children identify the rhyming words (low/bow/fro and shoulder/soldier).

Learning Centers

Art (Bow Art)

Encourage the children to make a collage using old bows. This is a great recycling activity. Provide some untied ribbon so they can create their own bows.

Discovery (Ear Equipment)

Place an assortment of ear items such as earrings, earmuffs, headphones, earplugs, and so on in the center. Encourage the children to explore the items. Discuss the different types of earrings. Encourage the children to try on the earrings.

Listening (Tell Me a Story)

Provide books and listening tapes for the children to enjoy. Talk with them about the importance of our ears. *What would we do if we couldn't hear? How would we communicate? Could we use the telephone?*

Science (Listen Carefully)

Place small playdough balls inside several plastic eggs. Encourage the children to roll the eggs across the floor. Discuss the wobbling motion of the eggs. Provide tops for the children to spin. Point out how the tops wobble when they slow down.

Outdoor Play or Music and Movement Activity

1. Play some marching music and encourage the children to march like Continental soldiers.
2. Sing along with "Do Your Ears Hang Low?" (*Where Is Thumbkin?* CD), "High-Low" (*I Am Special* CD, Thomas Moore), or "Do Your Ears Hang Low?" (*Walt Disney Records: Children's Favorite Songs Vol. 2* CD).

BRAIN CONNECTIONS

Our ears are responsible for about 30% of the stimuli that enters our brains for processing.

REFLECTIONS

How are the long ears on rabbits like the long ears on donkeys? How are they different?

Name some things you have used your ears for today.

Doodle-li-do

Doodle-li-do
(Tune: Traditional)

Please sing to me that sweet melody
Called the Doodle-li-do, Doodle-li-do.
I like the rest, but the part I like best
Goes Doodle-li-do, Doodle-li-do.
It's the simplest thing, there isn't much to it.
All you gotta do is Doodle-li-do it.
I like it so, wherever I go
It's the Doodle-li, Doodle-li-do.

Come on and Waddle-li-atcha, Waddle-li-atcha,
Waddle-li-o, Waddle-li-o.
Waddle-li-atcha, waddle-li-atcha
Waddle-li-o, Waddle-li-o.

It's the simplest thing, there isn't much to it.
All you gotta do is Doodle-li-do it.
I like it so, wherever I go
It's the Doodle-li-Doodle-li-do.

Perform these movements in rhythm with the music. Clap thighs twice. Clap hands twice. Cross hands in front of you four times (left hand on top twice, then right hand on top twice). Touch nose then right shoulder with left hand. Touch nose then left s houlder with right hand. Move hands in "talking" motion just above shoulders, then above head. Repeat throughout the song.

THEME CONNECTIONS

Animal Sounds
Animals
Friends
Humor
Music
Sound and
    Movement
Sounds of Language
Things I Like/
    Favorite Things

Related Songs, Chants, and Rhymes

Fiddle-I-Fee (Tune: Traditional)

I had a cat, and the cat pleased me.
Fed my cat under yonder tree.
Cat went fiddle-i-fee.

I had a hen, and the hen pleased me.
Fed my hen under yonder tree.
Hen went chimmey chuck, chimmey chuck,
Cat went fiddle-i-fee.

I had a dog, and the dog pleased me.
Fed my dog under yonder tree.
Dog went bow-wow, bow-wow,
Hen went chimmey chuck, chimmey chuck,
Cat went fiddle-i-fee.

Polly Wolly Doodle (Tune: Traditional)

Oh, I went down south
For to see my Sal
Sing Polly wolly doodle all the day
My Sal, she is
A spunky gal,
Sing Polly wolly doodle all the day.

Chorus:
Fare thee well, fare thee well,
Fare thee well my fairy fay
For I'm going to Lou'siana
For to see my Susyanna
Sing Polly wolly doodle all the day.

Oh, my Sal, she is
A maiden fair,
Sing Polly wolly doodle all the day,
With curly eyes
And laughing hair,
Sing Polly wolly doodle all the day.

Chorus

Behind the barn,
Down on my knees
Sing Polly wolly doodle all the day.
I thought I heard
A chicken sneeze,
Sing Polly wolly doodle all the day.

Chorus

He sneezed so hard
With the whooping cough,
Sing Polly wolly doodle all the day.
He sneezed his head
And tail right off,
Sing Polly wolly doodle all the day.

Chorus

Literacy Activities

(Select one or two follow-up activities to do each time you sing a song or say a rhyme.)

Oral Language Development

1. Discuss the words that may be new vocabulary for the children, such as "melody" and "simplest."
2. Discuss nonsense words. Point out that "doodle-li-do," "waddle-li-atcha," and "waddle-li-o" are all nonsense words. They have a melodic (nice) sound, but they have no meaning. Encourage the children to play with the concept of nonsense words. You may be able to uncover nonsense words by making up rhyming words for the children's names.

Phonological Awareness

1. Write "doodle-li-do, doodle-li-do" on chart paper and point out the repetitive use of the letter "d." Remind the children that repeated letter sounds are called **alliteration**.

2. Encourage the children to make up rhyming words to go with "doodle-li" (e.g., oodle-li, poodle-li, noodle-li and so forth).

Learning Centers

Music (Melodies)

Explain that melodies are made up of musical notes. Provide a xylophone, guitar, or other musical instrument and encourage the children to explore the sounds of different musical notes.

Science (Tone Bottles)

Fill four glass bottles or jars with different amounts of water. Fill one bottle ¼ full, another bottle ½ full, a third bottle ¾ full, and the last bottle completely full. Provide a spoon and encourage the children to tap the bottles and listen to the tones each one makes. Explain that these tones, when played together, create a tune or a melody. Supervise this activity.

Snack (Noodles)

Make noodles for snack. Try using a variety of noodles, or use different toppings, such as grated cheese, butter, or tomato sauce.

Writing (Doodle, Noodle, Poodle)

Write the words "doodle," "noodle," and "poodle" on chart paper. Encourage the children to copy the words using magnetic letters. Show them how to write "oodle" and then add a "d", "n", or "p" to change the word. Some children will be able to write the words. Suggest that they write the words on index cards and add them to their Word Box (shoebox collection of words they can write).

Outdoor Play or Music and Movement Activity

1. Play Doodle, Doodle, Do as you would Duck, Duck, Goose. Have the children sit in a circle. One child is IT. IT walks around the outside of the circle, tapping each player on the head and saying, "Doodle." Eventually IT taps a player and says, "Do" instead. The tapped player chases IT around the circle. If she taps IT before they get around the circle, she gets to go back to her place. If she doesn't, she becomes the new IT and the game continues.

2. Sing along with "Doodley Do" (*Thinkable, Movable, Lovable Songs* CD, ProVideo Productions), "Fiddle-I-Fee" (*Three Little Kittens* CD, Kimbo), "Polly Wolly Doodle" (*Here Is Thumbkin!* CD, Kimbo), "Polly Wolly Doodle" (*Walt Disney Records: Children's Favorite Songs Vol. 2* CD), or "Rock-a-Doodle" (*A Whole Lot of Animals* CD, Joel Reese).

REFLECTIONS

Which sound do you prefer: "doodle-li-do" or "waddle-li-atcha"? Why?

What is your favorite song? Why?

Down by the Bay

Down by the Bay
(Tune: Traditional)

Down by the bay where the watermelons grow
Back to my home I dare not go.
For if I do my mother will say,
"Did you ever see a pig dancing the jig?"
Down by the bay.

Additional verses:

…*"Did you ever see a whale with a polka dot tail?"*…
…*"Did you ever see a bear combing his hair?"*…
…*"Did you ever see a moose kissing a goose?"*…
…*"Did you ever see a pig wearing a wig?"*…

Make up your own additional verses.

THEME CONNECTIONS
Animals
Parts of the Body
Humor
Insects
Ocean
Seasons

Related Songs, Chants, and Rhymes

Just Plant a Watermelon on My Grave (Tune: Traditional)

Just plant a little watermelon on my grave,
Let the juice (slurp, slurp) *trickle through.*
Just plant a little watermelon on my grave,
That's all I ask of you.
Now I've tasted fried chicken (rub tummy in circle)

SEE ALSO

"There's a Hole in
the Middle of
the Sea" p. 190
"To Market, To
Market" p. 196

And it's mighty, mighty fine,
But nothing can compare to a watermelon riiiiind.
Just plant a little watermelon on my grave,
Let the juice (slurp, slurp) *trickle through.*

She Waded in the Water (Tune: Battle Hymn of the Republic)

She waded in the water and she got her feet all wet,
She waded in the water and she got her feet all wet,
She waded in the water and she got her feet all wet,
But she didn't get her (clap, clap) *wet* (clap) *yet.* (clap)

Chorus:
Glory, glory, hallelujah!
Glory, glory, hallelujah!
Glory, glory, hallelujah!
But she didn't get her (clap, clap) *wet* (clap) *yet.* (clap)

She waded in the water and she got her ankles wet (3 times)
But she didn't get her (clap, clap) *wet* (clap) *yet.* (clap)

Chorus

She waded in the water and she got her knees all wet...
She waded in the water and she got her thighs all wet...
She waded in the water and she finally got it wet...
She finally got her bathing suit wet!

Literacy Activities

(Select one or two follow-up activities to do each time you sing a song or say a rhyme.)

Oral Language Development

1. Discuss the words in the song that may be new vocabulary for some children, such as "bay," "jig," and "watermelon."
2. Talk with the children about watermelons. *Where do they grow? What do they taste like?* Serve watermelon for snack, if possible.

Phonological Awareness

1. Encourage the children to help identify the rhyming words: bay/say, pig/jig, bear/hair, and whale/tail.

Letter Knowledge and Recognition

1. Write the words "pig" and "jig" on index cards. Ask the children which letters are alike and which letters are different in each word.

Learning Centers

Art (My Favorite Verse)

Let the children illustrate their favorite verse of the song or make an illustration for a new verse.

Games (Whale Tail)

Cut out a whale from gray construction paper or bulletin board paper. Cut his tail off and add some polka dots. Play Pin the Tail on the Whale as you would play Pin the Tail on the Donkey.

Science (Bee Work)

Place pictures of bees in the Science Center. Provide a magnifying glass so the children can look for details. Ask questions. *Can you find the bee's knees? How many knees does a bee have?*

Writing (Pig/Jig)

Give the children word cards with "pig" and "jig" written on them and a tray of sand. Encourage the children to use their index finger to write the words in the sand.

Some children will be able to write the words. Suggest that they write the words on index cards and add them to their Word Box (shoebox collection of words they can write).

Outdoor Play or Music and Movement Activity

1. Teach the children a Pig Jig (make up a dance). Play some "barnyard" (fiddle) music and kick up your heels!
2. Sing along with "Down by the Bay" (*Where Is Thumbkin?* CD, Kimbo) or "Down by the Bay" (*Singable Songs for the Very Young: Great With a Peanut Butter Sandwich* CD, Raffi).

REFLECTIONS

Who can remember some of the rhyming words we talked about today?

Which verse of the song do you like best? Why?

Five Fat Turkeys Are We

Five Fat Turkeys Are We
(Tune: Traditional)

Five fat turkeys are we,
We spent the night in a tree.
When the cook came around,
We couldn't be found
And that's why we're here, you see!

Oh, five fat turkeys are we,
We spent the night in a tree.
It sure does pay on Thanksgiving Day,
To sleep in the tallest tree!

Related Songs, Chants, and Rhymes

Mighty Fine Turkey

I'm a mighty fine turkey and I sing a fine song—
Gobble, gobble, gobble.
I strut around the barnyard all day long,
My head goes—bobble, bobble, bobble.
On Thanksgiving Day I run away with a—
Waddle, waddle, waddle.
So that on the day after my head will still—
Bobble, bobble, bobble.

Literacy Activities

(Select one or two follow-up activities to do each time you sing a song or say a rhyme.)

Oral Language Development

1. If teaching this song around Thanksgiving, invite the children to discuss what they will be having for Thanksgiving dinner.
2. Teach the children how to make the American Sign Language sign (appendix p. 241) for turkey.

THEME CONNECTIONS
Animals
Counting/Numbers
Holidays/Celebrations
Humor

SEE ALSO
"Over the River and Through the Woods" p. 163
"She'll Be Comin' 'Round the Mountain" p. 164

Phonological Awareness

1. Point out the rhyming words in the song (we/tree, around/found).
2. Discuss the sounds that turkeys make and point out that "gobble, gobble" is an example of **onomatopoeia**. Remind them that **onomatopoeia** words sound like the sound they are describing. Teach the children, "Mighty Fine Turkey" to introduce the sound.

Learning Centers

Discovery (Feather Race)

Make a masking tape start and finish line about 4" apart. Place two feathers on the start line. Provide straws, a paper towel tube, paper plates, and squeeze bottles to use as feather "pushers." Invite two children to each choose a pusher and then attempt to use it to move the feather from the start to the finish line. Explain that they cannot touch the feather with their pusher. The first child to get the feather to the finish line is the winner and can then compete against another challenger.

Games (Turkey Hunt)

Make several photocopies of turkeys. Hide the turkeys in the room and invite the children to find them. *How many did you find?* Encourage the children to take turns hiding and finding the turkeys.

Science (Drop the Feather)

Give the children a turkey feather (any feather will do if a turkey feather is not available). Provide a plastic bowl and challenge the children to hold the feather at nose level and drop it in the bowl. *What happens to the feather on the way down? Would it be easier to drop a bead in the bowl?* Encourage the children to try it and see.

Writing (Gobble)

Write the word "gobble" on several index cards and provide some tracing paper. Encourage the children to trace the word.

Outdoor Play or Music and Movement Activity

1. Show the children how to walk like a turkey. Encourage them to walk around the room or playground pretending to be turkeys.
2. Sing along with "Five Fat Turkeys Are We" (*Where Is Thumbkin?* CD, Kimbo) or "She'll Be Coming Around the Mountain" (*Songs Kids Love to Sing* CD, Thomas Moore).

REFLECTIONS

How are turkeys different from ducks and chickens?

How do you think the turkeys got up in the tree?

Do you think turkeys are really smart enough to know they can hide in a tree?

Five Little Ducks

Five Little Ducks
(Tune: Traditional)

Five little ducks went out one day
Over the hills and far away.
Mother duck called with a "Quack, quack, quack."
Four little ducks came swimming back.

Repeat, losing one more duck each time until you are left with one duck.
Have mother duck call and end with "five little ducks
came swimming back."

Related Songs, Chants, and Rhymes

Be Kind to Your Web-Footed Friends (Tune: Stars and Stripes Forever)

Be kind to your web-footed friends,
For a duck may be somebody's mother.
Be kind to the birds in the swamp,
For the weather is very damp
Oh, you may think that this is the end,
Well, it is!

THEME CONNECTIONS
Animal Sounds
Animals
Counting/Numbers

One Little Duck (Tune: Traditional)

One little duck went out to play
Down by the pond on a fine spring day.
Another one said, "That's fun to do!"
He joined in and that made two.

Two little ducks went out to play
Down by the pond on a fine spring day.
Another one said, "Hey, wait for me!"
He joined in and that made three.

Three little ducks went out to play
Down by the pond on a fine spring day.
Another one peeked 'round the old barn door.
He joined in that made four.

Four little ducks went out to play
Down by the pond on a fine spring day.
Another one saw them dip and dive.
He joined in and that made five.

Five little ducks went out to play,
Down by the pond on a fine spring day.
The mother duck wished they all would come back.
She called them home with a "quack, quack, quack."

SEE ALSO
"Downy Duck"
    p. 138
"Little Ducky
    Duddle" p. 137
"Over in the
    Meadow" p. 64
"Six White Ducks"
    p. 137

Literacy Activities

(Select one or two follow-up activities to do each time you sing a song or say a rhyme.)

Oral Language Development

1. Find out what the children know about ducks. *What do ducks look like? What colors are they? Where do they live? How do they move? What sounds do they make?* If photos are available, use them to stimulate discussion.
2. Teach the children to make the American Sign Language sign (appendix p. 239) for duck.

Phonological Awareness

1. Point out that "quack, quack, quack" is an example of **onomatopoeia**, a term used for words that sound like the sound they are describing.
2. Help the children identify the rhyming words in the song (play/away, quack/back).

Comprehension

1. Ask the children questions. *Why did the ducks come back when mother duck called? What do you think the ducks were doing on the other side of the hill? Have you ever not come when your mother or father called you? What were you doing?*

2. Ask the children how "Five Little Ducks" is different from the similar song, "One Little Duck."

Learning Centers

Art (Feather Painting)

Provide feathers to use as brushes and some tempera paint and paper. Encourage the children to try feather painting. *What is it like using a feather as a brush?*

Discovery (Megaphones)

Show the children how to roll a piece of paper to create a megaphone or provide empty paper towel tubes to use as megaphones. Ask the children why they think a megaphone helps make a voice louder. Ask them if they think the baby ducks might have heard their mother calling if she used a megaphone.

Gross Motor (Duck Feet)

Give the children swimming fins to use as duck feet. Encourage them to walk in the fins. Place a strip of masking tape on the floor and challenge the children to walk along a line. *Is it easy or difficult to walk with duck feet? Do you think it is difficult for ducks to walk?* Ask the children to try walking backwards. *Is it easier or more difficult? Why?*

Water Play (Ducky Float)

Provide rubber ducks for the sand and water table. If possible, provide seven ducks so the children can re-enact the song.

Outdoor Play or Music and Movement Activity

1. Play Duck, Duck, Goose. Children sit in a circle. One child (IT) walks around the outside of the circle, tapping each player on the head and saying, "Duck." Eventually IT taps a player and says, "Goose" instead. The tapped player gets up and chases IT around the circle. If she taps IT before they get around the circle, she gets to go back to her place. If she doesn't, she becomes the new IT and the game continues.
2. Try some of these music and movement ideas:
    - Teach the children how to waddle like a duck. Encourage them children to find a partner and have a duck race.
    - Sing along with "Five Little Ducks" (*Where Is Thumbkin?* CD, Kimbo).

REFLECTIONS

How are ducks like turkeys and chickens? How are they different?

When people are describing how ducks walk, sometimes they say that they waddle. Can you think of a better word to describe how ducks walk?

Five Little Fishes Swimming in the Sea

Five Little Fishes Swimming in the Sea
(Tune: Over in the Meadow)

No little fishes swimming in the sea
Splishing and a-splashing and rocking to the beat.
Everybody wave 'cause don't you know
Here comes a fish and away we go.

One little fish swimming in the sea
Splishing and a-splashing and rocking to the beat.
Here comes another fish so say, "Hello."
Two little fishes swimming in a row.

Two little fishes swimming in the sea
Splishing and a-splashing and rocking to the beat.
Here comes another fish so say, "Hello."
Three little fishes swimming in a row.

Three little fishes...

Four little fishes...

Five little fishes swimming in the sea.
Everybody wave 'cause don't you know,
Five little fishes have got to go
Oh-ahh! Away they go. Yeah!

THEME CONNECTIONS
Animal Sounds
Animals
Counting/Numbers
Families
Nature

Related Songs, Chants, and Rhymes

Counting Rhyme

One, two, three, four, five,
I caught a fish alive.
Six, seven, eight, nine, ten,
I let it go again.
Why did I let him go?
Because he bit my finger so.

Over in the Meadow (Tune: Traditional)

Over in the meadow, in the sand, in the sun,
Lived an old mother frog and her little froggie one.
"Croak!" said the mother; "I croak!" said the one,
So they croaked and they croaked in the sand, in the sun.

Over in the meadow, in the stream so blue,
Lived an old mother fish and her little fishies two.
"Swim!" said the mother; "We swim!" said the two.
So they swam and they swam in the stream so blue.

Over in the meadow, on a branch of the tree,
Lived an old mother bird and her little birdies three.
"Sing!" said the mother; "We sing!" said the three,
And they sang and they sang on a branch of the tree.

Literacy Activities

(Select one or two follow-up activities to do each time you sing a song or say a rhyme.)

Oral Language Development

1. Discuss "rocking to the beat." Play some music and demonstrate. Have the children demonstrate how a fish might rock to the beat.
2. Try singing the song substituting the word "duckies" for fishes and "pond" for sea. *How does a duckie "rock to the beat?" Which version of the song do you like better?*
3. If photos of fish are available, use them to stimulate discussion about fish. *Where do they live? What color are fish? How do fish move? How do they breathe?*
4. Teach the children to make the American Sign Language sign (appendix p. 239) for fish.

SEE ALSO

"Michael Finnegan" p. 35

"There's a Hole in the Middle of the Sea" p. 190

"Wynken, Blynken, and Nod" p. 108

Letter Knowledge and Recognition

1. Write the word "fish" on chart paper or with magnetic letters on a magnetic board. Spell the word as you place the letters. Show the children how to make the word "fish" into "fishes." Make sure they understand that the word "fishes" is a made-up word. Explain that the plural word for fish is "fish," and that there are some words in our language that don't need an "s" when referring to more than one of something. Sheep is another example. If we said, "Sheeps," it would be a made-up word. Give some other examples. Ask children to brainstorm ideas for why the song uses the made-up word "fishes" instead of "fish" (for example, it sounds funny, it makes the sentence fit the music, it sounds like children talking, and so on).

Phonological Awareness

1. Point out that "splish" and "splash" are words that sound like the sound they are describing. They are examples of **onomatopoeia**. Ask the children to think of other sounds that water might make.

Learning Centers

Blocks (Fish Pond)

Cut out a "pond" from blue butcher paper or a blue sheet and several fish from construction paper. Also provide rubber ducks and, if available, other pond dwellers such as frogs or props such as lily pads. Encourage the children to construct a pond. Use the cardboard cylinder from a coat hanger (or a cardboard roll from wrapping paper) to make a fishing pole. Place a magnet on the string on the fishing pole and a paper clip on the nose of each fish. Invite the children to fish.

Discovery (Twirly Fish)

Make "twirly fish." Cut a strip of paper 1 ½" x 11". Lay the strip in front of you horizontally. Make a slit halfway through the width of the strip, 2" from the left end of the strip (top toward bottom). Make the same type of cut on the right end (bottom toward top). Insert the slits into each other to create a twirly fish. Encourage the children to hold the fish "nose high" and drop them. They will twirl to the ground. Ask the children if they think this is one way a fish might "rock to the beat."

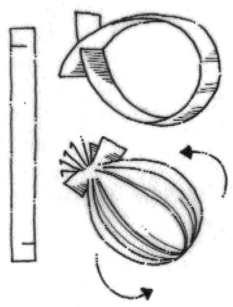

Math (Fish Count)

Cut out fish from construction paper or acetate. Use a paper clip to clip fish together in sets. Make a set of 1, 2, 3, 4, and 5. Tie catgut to five paper clips that you have reshaped into an "s" shape. Attach each set of fish to the other end of the paper clip. Write the numerals 1 to 5 on index cards. Encourage the children to clip the sets of fish to the corresponding numeral card.

Writing (I Can Spell "Fish")

Give the children magnetic letters and encourage them to write the word "fish." Show them how to change only the first letter to change the word to "wish" and "dish."

Write the word "fish" on index cards and let the children glue "scales" (clear sequins) over the letters. Some children will be able to write the words. Suggest that they write the word on an index card and add it to their Word Box (shoebox collection of words they can write).

Outdoor Play or Music and Movement Activity

1. Play Fish Games. Take a jump rope outdoors for jumping rope. Make a hopscotch grid and play hopscotch.
2. When indoors, play some music and encourage the children to pretend to be fish "rocking to the beat."
3. Sing along with "Five Fish Swimming in the Sea" (*Dr. Jean Sings Silly Songs* CD, Jean Feldman).

BRAIN CONNECTIONS

Fish is one of the best "brain foods." It is full of protein, which helps the brain think alertly and clearly.

REFLECTIONS

Have you ever been fishing? Did you catch a fish?

How would the song be different if we substituted the word "froggies" for "fishes?" Would we need to change the word "sea?"

Five Little Speckled Frogs

Five Little Speckled Frogs
(Tune: Traditional)

Five little speckled frogs

Sitting on a speckled log

Eating some most delicious bugs.

Yum! Yum!

One jumped into the pool,

Where it was nice and cool.

Now there are four little speckled frogs.

Burr-ump!

Repeat, counting down until there are no little speckled frogs.

Related Songs, Chants, and Rhymes

Hanky Panky (Tune: Traditional)

Down by the banks of the Hanky Panky,

Where the bullfrogs jump from bank to banky

With an Eep! Eep! Ope! Ope!

Knee flop-i-dilly and ker-plop.

THEME CONNECTIONS

Animal Sounds

Animals

Amphibians

Counting/Numbers

Sounds of Language

SEE ALSO

"Frog Went A-
      Courtin'" p. 70
"Over in the
      Meadow" p. 64

Hear the Lively Song (Tune: Traditional)

Hear the lively song
Of the frogs in yonder pond.
Crick, crick, crickety-crick,
Burr-rump!

Literacy Activities

(Select one or two follow-up activities to do each time you sing a song or say a rhyme.)

Oral Language Development

1. Discuss some of the words introduced in the song that may be new vocabulary for the children (such as "delicious," "croak," and "speckled").

2. Find out what the children know about frogs. *What color are frogs? Where do they live? How do they move? What sounds do they make?* If photos are available, use them to stimulate discussion.

3. Invite the children to think of additional words, other than speckled, to describe the frogs in the song (for example, jumping frogs, yellow frogs, hungry frogs, and so forth). Sing the song and insert some of their ideas. You may want to clap out the syllables in "speckled" to help the children realize that their new word has two syllables.

4. Teach the children how to make the American Sign Language sign (appendix p. 240) for frog.

Phonological Awareness

1. Help children identify the rhyming words in the song. Can they think of other words that rhyme with "cool" and "pool"? *What about the words "frog" and "log"?*

2. Ask the children questions about the sounds the frogs make in the various songs. *Does the sound the frogs make in "Five Little Speckled Frogs" (croak, croak) sound like the sound real-life frogs make? What about the sounds in "Hear the Lively Song" (crick, crick, crickety crick, bur-rump)? What about the sounds in "Hanky Panky" (Eep! Eep! Ope! Ope! knee flop-i-dilly and ker-plop)?* Explain to the children that when words sound like the sound they are describing, they are called **onomatopoeic** words.

Letter Knowledge and Recognition

1. Write the word "frog" on a piece of paper. Encourage the children to use magnetic letters to copy the word. If the children are ready, help them use magnetic letters to write a word that describes a frog.

Learning Centers

Art (Speckled Frogs)

Invite children to use a crayon to draw a frog, and then use green or brown tempera paint to splatter some speckles onto their frogs. Let them name their frog. With their permission, write the name of their frog on their paper. Some children may prefer that you write the name of the frog on the back of their paper.

Gross Motor (Lily Pad Jump)

Cut out green lily pads from construction paper and encourage the children to jump from pad to pad. Ask questions. *Are you able to jump as far as a frog can jump? Which parts of your body do you use when jumping?*

Science (Frog Inspection)

Obtain a live frog. Display with a magnifying glass. Encourage the children to look at the texture of the frog's skin. *What color are the frog's eyes? What do his feet look like? Which legs does he use for jumping?* If a real frog is not available, provide a photograph.

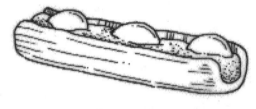

Snack (Frogs on a Log)

Invite the children to follow the rebus directions to make Frogs on a Log (see appendix p. 229). Ask questions as they work. *Have you ever eaten grapes and peanut butter together before? Do you think the grapes look like frogs?*

Outdoor Play or Music and Movement Activities

1. Invite the children to try some "frog jumps" (broad jumps). Place a piece of tape on the ground to represent a start line. Place a beanbag two feet away from the start line to mark the distance a speckled frog might jump. Encourage the children to stand on the tape and then jump as far as they are able. *Can children jump as far as a frog?* Point out that frogs have powerful back legs. *How are frog legs different from human legs?*

2. Try some of the following music and movement ideas:
    *   Invite the children to listen to "The Frog Family" (*Thomas Moore Sings the Family* CD, Thomas Moore). Ask volunteers to pretend to be the baby frog, mother frog, and father frog.
    *   Sing along with "Five Little Frogs" (*Singable Songs for the Very Young* CD, Raffi).

BRAIN CONNECTIONS

Using lesson themes and topics that are naturally interesting to children enhances the probability that you will have their attention. Most children are fascinated by frogs. However, if a child is afraid of frogs, be cautious. Fear interferes with the ability to pay attention. The brain is too busy working on ways to ensure safety and security.

REFLECTIONS

What did you learn about frogs today? What color are they? How do they move? Who can describe the sounds frogs make?

Do you think a frog would make a good pet? Why or why not?

Frog Went A-Courtin'

Frog Went A-Courtin'
(Tune: Traditional)

Frog went a-courtin' and he did ride.
Uh-huh; uh-huh.
Frog went a-courtin' and he did ride
With a sword and scabbard by his side.
Uh-huh; uh-huh.

He rode up to Miss Mousie's den.
Uh-huh; uh-huh.
He rode up to Miss Mousie's den,
Said "Please, Miss Mousie, won't you let me in?"
Uh-huh; uh-huh.

"First, I must ask my Uncle Rat.
Uh-huh; uh-huh.
"First I must ask my Uncle Rat
And see what he will say to that."
Uh-huh; uh-huh.

"Miss Mousie, won't you marry me?"
Uh-huh; uh-huh.
"Miss Mousie, won't you marry me
Way down under the apple tree?"
Uh-huh; uh-huh.

"Where will the wedding supper be?"
Uh-huh; uh-huh.
"Where will the wedding supper be?"
"Under the same old apple tree."
Uh-huh; uh-huh.

"What will the wedding supper be?"
Uh-huh; uh-huh.
"What will the wedding supper be?"
"Hominy grits and black-eyed peas."
Uh-huh; uh-huh.

The first come in was a bumblebee.
Uh-huh; uh-huh.
The first come in was a bumblebee
With a big bass fiddle on his knee.
Uh-huh; uh-huh.

The last come in was a mockingbird.
Uh-huh; uh-huh.
The last come in was a mockingbird
Who said, "This marriage is absurd."
Uh-huh; uh-huh.

THEME CONNECTIONS

Animals
Amphibians
Boats and Ships
Emotions
Families
Humor
Real and Make-
   Believe
Sun, Moon, Stars

70

Related Songs, Chants, and Rhymes

Fiddle Dee Dee

Fiddle dee dee, fiddle dee dee,
The fly has married the bumblebee.
They went to the church,
And married was she.
The fly has married the bumblebee.

The Owl and the Pussycat
by Edward Lear

The owl and the pussycat went to sea
In a beautiful pea-green boat.
They took some honey, and plenty of
*   money*
Wrapped in a five-pound note.

The owl looked up to the stars above
And sang to a small guitar,
"O, lovely pussy, o pussy my love,
What a beautiful pussy you are, you are
What a beautiful pussy you are!"

Pussy said to the owl, "You elegant fowl,
How charmingly sweet you sing.
O, let us be married, too long we have
*   tarried,*
But what shall we do for a ring?"

They sailed away for a year and a day
To the land where the Bongtree grows.
And there in a wood a Piggywig stood
With a ring in the end of his nose, his nose,
With a ring in the end of his nose.

"Dear Pig, are you willing to sell for one
*   shilling*
Your ring?" Said the Piggy, "I will."
So they took it away and were married
*   next day*
By the turkey who lives on the hill.

They dined on mince and slices of quince
Which they ate with a runcible spoon;
And hand in hand on the edge of the sand
They danced by the light of the moon, the
*   moon,*
They danced by the light of the moon.

SEE ALSO
"A Tisket, A Tasket"
    p. 181
"Five Little
    Speckled Frogs"
    p. 67
"Hanky Panky"
    p. 71
"Hear the Lively
    Song" p. 68
"K-K-K-Katy"
    p. 135
"Old Gray Cat"
    p. 96
"Skidamarink"
    p. 181
"Three White Mice"
    p. 96

Literacy Activities

(Select one or two follow-up activities to do each time you sing a song or say a rhyme.)

Oral Language Development

1. Help define new words that may be new vocabulary for the children, such as "sword," "scabbard," "courting," "hominy grits," "black-eyed peas," "absurd," and "bass fiddle."

2. Find out what the children know about frogs and mice. *What color are frogs? Where do they live? How do they move? What sounds do they make?* If photos are available, use them to stimulate discussion.

3. Tell the children that "Frog Went A-Courtin'" is a **ballad.** Explain that songs that tell a story are called **ballads.** *Can you think of another song we know that is a ballad?* ("Green Grass Grew all Around" and "The Fox")

Comprehension

1. Ask the children questions to assess their understanding of the event described by the song. *Do you think a frog and a mouse could really marry? Why? Why not? Where would they live? What would they eat?*

Print Awareness

1. Ask the children to make a guest list of other animal friends a frog and a mouse might invite to their wedding. Make a guest list. Discuss the purpose of a guest list. Ask the children if they make guest lists for their birthday parties.

Learning Centers

Blocks (Come to My Pad)

Cut a large green lily pad from butcher paper and place it on the floor. Tell the children that this is where Frog and Mousie will live. Encourage children to build some furniture on the pad that will be appropriate for the home of a frog and a mouse. *What kind of bed will they sleep in? What will their kitchen look like?*

Cooking (Hominy Grits)

Prepare hominy grits. Discuss what the grits look like before they are cooked and after they are cooked. Ask questions. *How do they taste? Have you eaten grits before?*

Dramatic Play (Here Comes the Bride)

Place wedding props (e.g., a veil, rings, bouquet, and so forth) in the Dramatic Play Center. Encourage the children to enact a wedding.

Language (Mouse Den Reading Nook)

Create a mouse den. Cut an arched opening in the side of a large box. Toss pillows inside and provide a flashlight and some books for reading. Ask the children questions about where mice live. *Is the mouse den cozy? What makes it cozy? Does it make a good reading area? Why? Why not?*

Outdoor Play or Music and Movement Activity

1. Invite the children to play Leap Frog. Select one child to be the "frog." Ask the other children to get on their hands and knees and crouch down. Invite the frog to leap over the children by placing her hands on the back of each child for support while straddling her legs around the child's body.
2. Sing along with "Frog Went a-Courtin'" (*Where Is Thumbkin?* CD, Kimbo), "Froggie Went a-Courting" (*Rockin' Rhymes and Good Ol' Times* CD), or "Froggie Went a-Courting" (*Walt Disney Records: Children's Favorite Songs Vol. 4* CD).

Fuzzy Caterpillar

Fuzzy Caterpillar
(Tune: Traditional)

A fuzzy caterpillar went out for a walk.
His back went up and down.
He crawled and he crawled,
And he crawled and he crawled
'Til he crawled all over town.
He wasn't disappointed
Not a bit to be a worm.
Not a tear was in his eye
Because he knew what he'd become,
A very, very pretty butterfly.

Make a Caterpillar/Butterfly Puppet (appendix p. 235) to use with the song.
Turn a brown or black sock inside out. Glue or sew two wiggle eyes onto the toe of
the sock. Then turn the sock right side out, and glue or sew two wiggle eyes on the
toe and two felt wings midway up the sock. Sewing on the wings and eyes makes the
puppet more durable.

Related Songs, Chants, and Rhymes

Caterpillar

Who's that ticklin' my back? said the wall, (crawl fingers up arm)
"Me," said a small caterpillar, "I'm learning to crawl."

Metamorphosis

I'm an egg (curl up in fetal position)
I'm an egg
I'm an egg, egg, egg!

I'm a worm (open up and wiggle on the ground)
I'm a worm
I'm a wiggly, humpty worm!

**THEME
CONNECTIONS**
Animals
Insects

I'm a cocoon (curl up in a fetal position with hands over the face)
I'm a cocoon
I'm a round, silk cocoon!

I'm a butterfly (stand and fly around using arms for wings)
I'm a butterfly
I'm a grand and glorious butterfly!

Pretty Butterfly

Yesterday I went to the field.
I saw a beautiful butterfly. (hold hands in front of face as if holding and
  studying a butterfly)
But on seeing me so close,
It flew away ever so quickly. (make fluttering movements)

Literacy Activities

(Select one or two follow-up activities to do each time you sing a song or say a rhyme.)

Oral Language Development

1. Find out what children know about caterpillars and butterflies. *What color are they? Where do they live? How do they move? What sounds do they make?* If photos are available, use them to stimulate discussion.
2. Ask the children if they know what it is called when a caterpillar turns into a butterfly (metamorphosis). If no one knows, describe the process of metamorphosis. You may want to use a caterpillar/butterfly puppet (appendix p. 235) to demonstrate metamorphosis.
3. Have the children act out the rhyme, "Metamorphosis."

Comprehension

1. Ask questions. *Why was the caterpillar not disappointed he was a worm? How do caterpillars move? How do butterflies move?*

Learning Centers

Construction (Caterpillar Pets)

Give each child half of a paper egg carton. Provide tempera paint, pipe cleaners (antennae), and buttons or wiggle eyes. Encourage the children to construct their own caterpillar. Encourage them to give their caterpillar a name. Write the names on the inside of their creations.

Dramatic Play (Puppet Play)

Make a caterpillar/butterfly puppet (see appendix p. 235). Encourage the children to use the puppet to demonstrate metamorphosis. Encourage them to describe the process as they change the puppet from egg to caterpillar to butterfly.

Fine Motor (Caterpillar Pick-Up)

Cut several pieces of thick brown or black yarn into 2" segments. Place them on the floor. Give the children a pair of tweezers and a bucket. Challenge them to pick up the caterpillars with the tweezers and place them in the bucket.

Writing (Fuzzy)

Cut out the letters to spell "fuzzy" from fake fur.
Encourage the children to trace over the letters with their fingers. Provide magnetic letters for the children to use to copy the word, if desired.

Outdoor Play or Music and Movement Activity

1. Play some classical music. Provide colorful crepe paper streamers (2' strips) or scarves. Encourage the children to dance like butterflies.
2. Sing along with "Fuzzy Caterpillar" (*Thinkable, Movable, Lovable Songs* CD, ProVideo Productions).

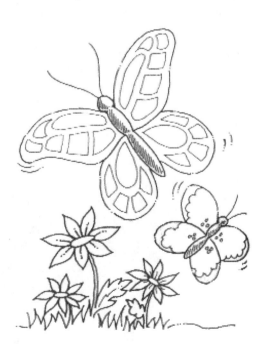

REFLECTIONS

Why did Fuzzy Caterpillar not mind being a worm? Why would he not want to be a worm if he wasn't going to become a butterfly?

If you had a caterpillar as a temporary pet (one we watch for a day), what would you name it? When it turned into a caterpillar, would his name still suit him? Will Fuzzy still be a good name for the caterpillar when he changes into a butterfly? Why? Why not?

Going on a Bear Hunt

Going on a Bear Hunt

(Leader says a line—others repeat. Pat on thighs in rhythm.)

Would you like to go on a bear hunt?

Okay—all right—come on—let's go!

Open the gate—close the gate. (clap hands)

Coming to a bridge—can't go over it—can't go under it.

Let's cross it. (thump chest with fists)

Coming to a river—can't go over it—can't go under it.

Let's swim it. (swim)

Coming to a tree—can't go over it—can't go under it.

Let's climb it. (climb up)

No bears! (climb down)

Coming to a wheat field—can't go over it—can't go under it.

Let's go through it! (rub palms together to make swishing noise)

Oh! Oh! I see a cave—it's dark in here. (cover eyes)

I see two eyes—I feel something furry. (reach out hand)

It's a bear!

Let's go home! (run in place)

(Describe and repeat above actions in reverse using fast motions.)

Slam the gate! (clap hands)

We made it!

THEME CONNECTIONS

Animals

Emotions

Rivers

Spatial
    Relationships

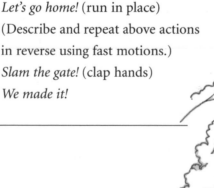

Related Songs, Chants, and Rhymes

A-Hunting We Will Go (Tune: The Farmer in the Dell)
A-hunting we will go,
A-hunting we will go.
We'll catch a little fox,
And put him in a box.
And then we'll let him go.

The Bear Went Over the Mountain
(Tune: For He's a Jolly Good Fellow)
The bear went over the mountain,
The bear went over the mountain,
The bear went over the mountain
To see what he could see.

And all that he could see,
And all that he could see,
Was the other side of the mountain,
The other side of the mountain,
The other side of the mountain,
Was all that he could see.

Going on a Safari by Pam Schiller
(This is an echo story to which a new verse is cumulatively added each time.)
I'm going on safari, and I'm not afraid. (children echo)
Got my camera and my water by my side. (echo, adding a new verse)
I'm going on safari, and I'm not afraid.
Got my camera and my water and my clothes by my side. (echo, adding a new verse)
. . . and my friends . . .
. . . and my money . . .
. . . and my food . . .

Going on a Trail Ride by Pam Schiller
(Suit actions to words. Leader says a line—others repeat.)
We're going on a trail ride.
Want to come along?
Well, then, come on.
Let's get ready!

Got to rope and brand the cattle.
Let's rope—stick on the brand.
Got to load up the chuck wagon.
Get the blankets and the food.
Don't forget the water—got to water our horses.

SEE ALSO
"There Once Were Three Brown Bears" p. 203
"Three Bears Rap" p. 202

Slurp, slurp.
Ready to go.
Now jump on your horse.
Let's go. (children hold horse reins and clip clop between verses)

Look! There's a river.
Can't go over it—can't go under it—can't go around it.
We'll have to go through it.

Look! There's some cactus.
Can't go under it—can't go over it—can't go through it.
We'll have to go around it.

Look! There's a mountain.
Can't go through it—can't go under it—can't go around it.
We'll have to go over it. (lean back)

Look! There's a wagon train.
Can't go through it—can't go under it—can't go over it.
We'll have to go around it.
(Optional: Stop here and sing some songs with the people on the wagon train.)

Look! There's the town!
Just what we are looking for!
Let's hurry! Get along, little dogies! (ride fast)
We're almost there. (continue to ride fast)
Civilization at last!

Going on a Whale Watch by Pam Schiller

We're going on a whale watch. (leader says first verse alone)
Want to come along? (children answer yes)
Well, come on then.
Let's go! (stand and walk in place)

(Leader says a line—others repeat.)
Look! There's our boat.
Can't go over it.
Can't go under it.
Can't go around it.
We'll need to get on it. (pretend to walk onto boat, and locate a good place
    to stand. Shade eyes as if watching for a whale and begin tapping fingers as if
    impatiently waiting.)

Look! There's a ship.
Can't go over it.

Can't go under it.
Can't go through it.
We'll have to go around it. (pretend to steer around the ship and then resume tapping fingers and watching for a whale)

Look! There's an iceberg.
Can't go over it.
Can't go under it.
Can't go through it.
We'll have to go around it. (pretend to steer around the iceberg and then resume tapping fingers and looking for a whale)

Look! There's a spout of water.
Is it a whale?
Ooh, I think it might be. (look straight ahead, shade eyes and squint)
I see a huge head.
Wonder what it is.

I see a tail.
It's big.
It's a whale! We found a whale!
Look out, here comes a s-p-l-a-s-h! (duck)
Too late. We're soaked! (pretend to wipe water from face)

Literacy Activities

(Select one or two follow-up activities to do each time you sing a song or say a rhyme.)

Oral Language Development

1. Discuss words that might be new to the children (such as "wheat field," "cave," "hunt," and so on).
2. Call attention to the spatial words ("over," "under," "around," and "through") in the chant. Place a block or carpet square in the middle of the floor and ask a volunteer to demonstrate each spatial word.
3. Provide photos of bears, if available, and use them to stimulate discussion about the characteristics and habitats of bears.
4. Teach the children the American Sign Language sign (appendix p. 239-240) for bear and horse.

Phonological Awareness

1. Discuss the sounds that are used with the chant, such as "splash" for the river and "swish" for the wheat field. Point out that these words are examples of **onomatopoeia**.

2. Talk about the sounds that you make with your body as you recite the chant. *Does patting your thighs with your hands sound like feet walking? Does the sound of brushing your hands together sound like walking through tall grass?*

Learning Centers

Dramatic Play (Find the Bear)

Using nature magazines or the Internet, find pictures of bears. Make photocopies and hide them around the center. Encourage the children to find the bears. If available, provide props including a hunting hat, flashlight, backpack, and so on. *What did you encounter on your hunt?* Make a cave by spreading a blanket over a table or a couple of chairs. Provide some stuffed bears to be cave dwellers. *What is it like inside the cave?*

Language (The Three Bears)

Using a storybook of "Goldilocks and the Three Bears," create your own flannel board pieces out of felt. Encourage the children to retell the story, including sound effects.

Math (Where's the Bear?)

Make photocopies of bears from nature magazines or books. Reduce the size when copying so that the bear is small enough to fit inside a small matchbox. Cover several matchboxes with contact paper and place the bears in the boxes. Ask the children to remove the bears from the boxes and place them in as many locations in relation to the box as they can. For example, they may put their bear on top of the box, under the box, beside the box, inside the box, far away from the box, and so forth. Encourage them to describe the location of the bear as they move him, emphasizing the spatial words (on, in, near, and so on).

Science (Bears Up Close)

Provide photos of bears. Encourage the children to take a good look at the photos. *How big are bears? What do their teeth look like? What do their claws look like? Why do they spend time in caves?*

Outdoor Play or Music and Movement Activity

1. Play Bear Hunt. Hide several stuffed bears or a paper bears on the playground and encourage the children to find them.
2. Sing along with "A-Hunting We Will Go" (*Walt Disney Records: Children's Favorite Songs Vol. 3* CD), "Bear Went Over the Mountain" (*Dr. Jean Sings Silly Songs* CD, Jean Feldman), or "The Cool Bear Hunt" (*Dr. Jean Sings Silly Songs* CD, Jean Feldman).

REFLECTIONS

Have you ever seen a real bear? Where? What was it like?

Why do you think the bear was in the cave? Was he sleeping? Why?

How do you feel when someone wakes you up before you are ready to wake up?

The Grand Old Duke of York

The Grand Old Duke of York
(Tune: Traditional)

The grand old Duke of York (salute)

He had ten thousand men. (hold up ten fingers)

He marched them up to the top of the hill, (point up)

And he marched them down again. (point down)

And when they're up, they're up. (stand tall)

And when they're down, they're down. (squat)

But when they're only halfway up,
    (stand with knees bent)

They're neither up nor down. (open arms and shrug)

Related Songs, Chants, and Rhymes

Where Do You Wear Your Ears?

Where do you wear your ears?

Underneath your hat?

Where do you wear your ears?

Yes ma'am, just like that.

Where do you wear your ears?

Say where, you sweet, sweet child.

Where do you wear your ears?

On both ends of my smile!

Yankee Doodle (Tune: Traditional)

Yankee Doodle came to town

Riding on a pony.

He stuck a feather in his cap

And called it macaroni.

Father and I went down to camp

Along with Captain Gooding,

And there we saw the men and boys

As thick as hasty pudding.

THEME CONNECTIONS

Animals

Counting/Numbers

Holidays/Celebrations

Humor

Movement

Opposites

Parts of the Body

Patriotism

Spatial
    Relationships

SEE ALSO

"Do Your Ears
    Hang Low?"
    p. 49

"Humpty Dumpty"
    p. 104

Yankee Doodle keep it up,
Yankee Doodle dandy,
Mind the music and the step
And with the girls be handy.

There was Captain Washington
Upon a strapping stallion,
A-giving orders to his men
I guess there was a million.

Yankee Doodle keep it up,
Yankee Doodle dandy,
Mind the music and the step
And with the girls be handy.

Literacy Activities

(Select one or two follow-up activities to do each time you sing a song or say a rhyme.)

Oral Language Development

1. Discuss words that may be new vocabulary to the children, such as "grand," "Duke," "ten thousand" and "half."
2. Ask a volunteer to demonstrate the positional words: up, down, and halfway up.

Print Awareness

1. Write the number 10,000 on chart paper. Explain that this is a number and is made up of numerals. Explain that numerals are different from letters. Have the children identify the numerals if they are able. Ask the children to count the ones in the number, then count the zeros.

Learning Centers

Blocks (Up and Down)

Create an inclined plank. Encourage children to roll cars up and down the plank. Ask questions. *Is it easier to get the cars up the plank or down the plank? Do you think the army men found it easier to march up the hill or down the hill? Can you roll the car halfway up the plank?*

Discovery (Lights Up and Down)

Provide flashlights and encourage the children to shine the light up the wall, down the wall, and halfway up the wall. Encourage them to use the flashlights as spotlights. Ask them to spotlight something that is up and something that is down. *Can you spotlight something that is halfway up the wall? How many things halfway up the wall can you find?*

Fine Motor (Hills)

Provide playdough and encourage the children to make hills. After they have made several hills, ask them to arrange the hills in order from tallest to smallest. Ask questions about the hills. *Have you ever seen hills? Were they high hills or low hills? Have you ridden over hills in your car before? Did it make your tummy feel funny?* Adjust your questions to address the terrain you feel the children will most likely be familiar with.

Science (Floaters and Droppers)

Provide some materials for the children to sort as floaters (feathers, tissues, cellophane) and droppers (buttons, spools, paper clips). Ask them to hold each item nose high and then drop it to the ground. *Which items float down? Which items drop? Do any items hang halfway?*

Outdoor Play or Music and Movement Activity

1. If there is a hill outdoors, encourage the children to march up the hill, down the hill, and halfway up the hill.
2. Sing along with "The Grand Old Duke of York" (*Where Is Thumbkin?* CD), "The Kids Go Marching" (*Thomas Moore Sings the Family* CD), "Yankee Doodle" (*Rockin' Rhymes and Good Ol' Times* CD), or "Yankee Doodle" (*Walt Disney Records: Children's Favorite Songs Vol. 2* CD).

REFLECTIONS

How long do you think it took the Duke of York's men to march up the hill? Which would take longer, marching up a high hill or marching up a low hill? Does it take longer to march halfway up the hill or all the way up the hill?

Can you find something in the room that is up? What about something that is down? Can you find something that is halfway up?

Gray Squirrel

Gray Squirrel (Tune: Traditional)

Gray squirrel, gray squirrel, (stand with your hands on bent knees)
Swish your bushy tail. (wiggle your behind)
Gray squirrel, gray squirrel, (stand with your hands on bent knees)
Swish your bushy tail. (wiggle your behind)
Wrinkle up your funny nose, (wrinkle your nose)
Hold an acorn in your toes. (pinch your index and thumb fingers together)
Gray squirrel, gray squirrel, (stand with hands on bent knees)
Swish your bushy tail. (wiggle your behind)

Related Songs, Chants, and Rhymes

I'm a Little Acorn Brown (Tune: I'm a Little Hunk of Tin)

I'm a little acorn brown,
Lying on the cold, cold ground.
Everyone walks over me,
That is why I'm cracked you see.
I'm a nut (click, click).
In a rut (click, click).
I'm a nut (click, click).
In a rut (click, click).

The Squirrel

Whisky, frisky,
Hippity hop,
Up he goes
To the tree top!

Whirly, twirly,
Round and round,
Down he scampers
To the ground.

Furly, curly,
What a tail!
Tall as a feather,
Broad as a sail!

Where's his supper?
In the shell;
Snappity, crackity,
Out it fell!

THEME CONNECTIONS
Animals
Colors
Parts of the Body
Seasons
Things That Go
　　Together

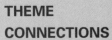

Literacy Activities

(Select one or two follow-up activities to do each time you sing a song or say a rhyme.)

Oral Language Development

1. Discuss words that may be new vocabulary for the children (such as "bushy," "swish," and "acorn").
2. Point out the action words (**verbs**) in the song—"swish," "wrinkle," and "hold." Explain that these words describe something the squirrel can do. Ask volunteers to demonstrate ways the squirrel might swish its tail, or wrinkle its nose, or hold an acorn in its toes. Encourage different kinds of responses.
3. Find out what children know about squirrels. *What color are squirrels? Where do they live? How do they move? What do they eat?* If photos of squirrels are available, use them to stimulate discussion.
4. Talk with the children about how squirrels use their bushy tails. Their tails actually serve a vital purpose, helping the squirrel balance when climbing and jumping, and slowing its fall when jumping from one object to another. When the squirrel becomes distressed, it will flick its tail back and forth and chatter loudly to warn its neighbors.
5. Teach the children to make the American Sign Language sign (appendix p. 241) for squirrel.

Phonological Awareness

1. Read the poem, "The Squirrel" (see Related Songs, Chants, and Rhymes). Help the children identify the rhyming words.
2. Discuss the rhyming words that also help describe the squirrel and its actions. Write pairs of rhyming words (whisky/frisky, whirly/twirly, and so on) on chart paper or on the chalkboard. Read each pair of words. Ask questions. *Which words describe the squirrel? Which words describe his actions? Which words are onomatopoeia words?* (whirly, twirly, snappity, crackity) Remind the children that **onomatopoeia** words sound like the action they describe.

Learning Centers

Art (Tail Brushes)

Create a squirrel-tail brush by wrapping a strip of fake fur around a long pipe cleaner and sealing it with glue. Provide tempera paint. Encourage the children to use the squirrel tail as a brush. *How does it work? Is it difficult to control? How is it like a real paintbrush? How is it different?*

Games (Pin the Tail on the Squirrel)

Enlarge the squirrel pattern (appendix p. 238). Cut it out and cut off the tail. Color and laminate. Encourage the children to play Pin the Tail on the Squirrel as they would play Pin the Tail on the Donkey. *Is it easier to pin the tail on wearing a blindfold or easier if you just close your eyes?* Ask the children if they can remember how squirrels use their tails.

Science (Squirrels and Their Teeth)

Perhaps the most unusual thing about squirrels is their teeth. Squirrels have rootless teeth that never stop growing. Because of this, they must continuously gnaw to wear the teeth down. If they do not gnaw, their teeth will grow so long the squirrel cannot eat! Provide photographs of squirrels so that the children can observe their long teeth. Give the children sandpaper and shells (or wood) to sand. Discuss how rough things can grind away surfaces when they are rubbed over them continuously. Explain that this is similar to the way squirrels grind down their long teeth.

Snack (Squirrel Food)

Provide several types of nuts (still in the shell). Show the children how to use a nutcracker to crack nuts. Discuss how squirrels use their teeth as nutcrackers and explain why it is not a good idea for us to use our teeth as nutcrackers. Invite the children to taste each type of nut. (**Warning**: Some children are allergic to nuts and some may have trouble swallowing nuts. Nuts can present a choking hazard. Check allergies and supervise this activity closely.)

Outdoor Play or Music and Movement Activity

1. Play Drop the Nut as you would play Drop the Handkerchief. Choose one child to be IT while the other children sit in a circle facing the center. The child who is IT skips or walks around the outside of the circle and casually drops a nut behind one of the children. This child picks up the nut and chases IT around the circle. IT tries to run around the circle and sit in the second child's spot without being tagged. If IT is not tagged, then he sits in his new spot in the circle and the child with the handkerchief is now IT. If IT is tagged, then he is IT for another round.

2. Sing along with "Gray Squirrel" (*Where Is Thumbkin?* CD, Kimbo), "Gray Squirrel" (*Thinkable, Movable, Lovable Songs* CD, ProVideo Productions), or "I'm a Nut" (*Keep on Singing and Dancing* CD, Jean Feldman).

BRAIN CONNECTIONS

Nuts are a good brain food because they are high in protein. Protein boosts alertness and mental performance.

REFLECTIONS

How do squirrels crack the nuts before they eat them? How do they get the nuts out of the shell?

How are squirrels like cats? How are they different?

The Green Grass Grew All Around

The Green Grass Grew All Around
(Tune: Traditional)

In the park there was a hole,
Oh, the prettiest hole you ever did see.
A hole in the park,
A hole in the ground,
And the green grass grew all around, all around,
And the green grass grew all around.

And in that hole there was a sprout,
Oh, the prettiest sprout you ever did see.
Sprout in the hole,
Hole in the ground,
And the green grass grew all around, all around,
And the green grass grew all around.

And from that sprout there grew a tree,
Oh, the prettiest tree you ever did see.
Tree from a sprout,
Sprout in a hole,
Hole in the ground,
And the green grass grew all around, all around,
And the green grass grew all around.

And on that tree there was a branch,
Oh, the prettiest branch you ever did see.
Branch on a tree,
Tree from a sprout,
Sprout in a hole,
Hole in the ground,
And the green grass grew all around, all around,
And the green grass grew all around.

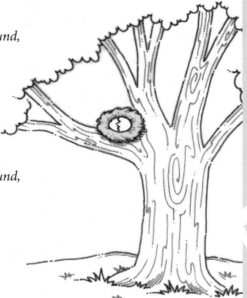

(continued on the next page)

THEME CONNECTIONS
Animals
Emotions
Growing Things
Nature
Sun, Moon, Stars
Things That Go
    Together
Weather

SEE ALSO

"The Ash Grove"
p. 115

"I Like Green" p. 44

And on that branch there was a nest,
Oh, the prettiest nest you ever did see.
Nest on a branch,
Branch on a tree,
Tree from a sprout,
Sprout in a hole,
Hole in the ground,
And the green grass grew all around,
    all around,
And the green grass grew all around.

And in that nest there was an egg,
Oh, the prettiest egg you ever did see.
Egg in a nest,
Nest on a branch,
Branch on a tree,
Tree from a sprout,
Sprout in a hole,
Hole in the ground,
And the green grass grew all around,
    all around,
And the green grass grew all around.

And in that egg there was a bird,
Oh, the prettiest bird you ever did see.
Bird in an egg,
Egg in a nest,
Nest on a branch,
Branch on a tree,
Tree from a sprout,
Sprout in a hole,
Hole in the ground,
And the green grass grew all around,
    all around,
And the green grass grew all around.

Related Songs, Chants, and Rhymes

Are You Growing? by Mike Artell/Pam Schiller
(Tune: Are You Sleeping?)

Are you growing,
Are you growing,
Little seeds, little seeds?
Are you getting sunlight?
Are you getting water?
Yes, I am.
Yes, I am.

Getting taller,
Getting taller,
Little plant, little plant.
I can count your leaves now.
I can count your leaves now.
One, two, three.
One, two, three.

Birdie, Birdie, Where Is Your Nest? (Tune: Traditional)

Birdie, birdie, where is your nest?
Birdie, birdie, where is your nest?
Birdie, birdie, where is your nest?
In the tree that I love best.

Great Green Gobs by Pam Schiller (Tune: Row, Row, Row Your Boat)

Great green gobs of grass,
Great green gobs of peas,
Grass and peas, peas and grass,
All in great green gobs.

Great green gobs of frogs,
Great green gobs of leaves,
Frogs and leaves, leaves and frogs,
All in great green gobs.

Tiny Seeds

Tiny seed planted just right, (tuck into a ball)
Not a breath of air, not a ray of light.
Rain falls slowly to and fro,
And now the seed begins to grow. (begin to unfold)
Slowly reaching for the light,
With all its energy, all its might.
The little seed's work is almost done,
To grow up tall and face the sun. (stand up tall with arms stretched out)

Under the Spreading Chestnut Tree (Tune: Traditional)

Under the spreading chestnut tree
There I held her on my knee.
We were happy yesiree.
Under the spreading chestnut tree.

Literacy Activities

(Select one or two follow-up activities to do each time you sing a song or say a rhyme.)

Oral Language Development

1. Help children define the words in the song that may be new vocabulary, such as "sprout" and "branch."
2. Discuss the prepositional words: "in," "on," "around," and "from." Use a block and a box to demonstrate each position.

Comprehension

1. Challenge the children to recall the sequence of events in the song.

Phonological Awareness

1. Write "Green Grass Grew" on chart paper or a chalkboard. Underline the "Gr" in each word and point out that the three words each start with the same two letters. Remind the children that when the words have the same beginning letters, it is called **alliteration**.

Learning Centers

Art (All Around)

Cut out a hole from the middle of a piece of butcher paper. Make the hole large enough for a child to sit in. Provide tempera paint and encourage the children to take turns sitting inside the hole and painting "all around" themselves. *What do you have to do to be able to paint all around the hole?*

Fine Motor (Green Grass Sweep)

Provide a tray of cut grass, a pastry brush, and a scoop. Encourage the children to sweep the grass into the scoop and dump it in a container. Ask children questions. *Who cuts the grass at your house? How does the person who cuts the grass at your house clean it up?*

Science (The Green Grass Grew)

Encourage the children to plant rye grass seeds in a paper cup. If desired, suggest that they paint a face on their cup. When the grass grows it will look like hair. Encourage the children to watch the seeds daily to record the growth. Show them how to use tally marks to count the number of days that pass before the grass sprouts. *How many days does it take for the grass to sprout? What helps the seeds grow?*

Writing (Green Grass Grew)

Invite the children to use magnetic letters to copy the words "Green Grass Grew." *What letter does each word begin with? What is the second letter in each word?* Some children will be able to write the words. Suggest that they write the words on index cards and add them to their Word Box (shoebox collection of words they can write).

Outdoor Play or Music and Movement Activity

1. Invite the children to act out the poem, "Tiny Seeds" (see Related Songs, Chants, and Rhymes).
2. Try some of the following music and movement ideas:
   - Play classical music and encourage the children to fly like birds.
   - Sing along with "The Green Grass Grew All Around" (*Here Is Thumbkin!* CD, Kimbo), "Chestnut Tree" (*Thinkable, Movable, Lovable Songs* CD, ProVideo Productions), or "The Green Grass Grew All Around" (*Walt Disney Records: Children's Favorite Songs Vol. 1* CD).

REFLECTIONS

Have you ever helped plant something? Tell us about it.

What do you think it would be like if the grass were blue and the sky were green? Would you like it better? Why? Why not?

Head, Shoulders, Knees, and Toes

Head, Shoulders, Knees, and Toes
(Tune: Traditional)

(touch body parts as they are mentioned in the song)

Head, shoulders, knees, and toes,

Knees and toes.

Head, shoulders, knees, and toes,

Knees and toes.

Eyes and ears and mouth and nose.

Head, shoulders, knees, and toes

Knees and toes!

Related Songs, Chants, and Rhymes

Head, Shoulders, Baby

Head, shoulders, baby 1, 2, 3.

Head, shoulders, baby 1, 2, 3.

Head, shoulders, head, shoulders,

Head, shoulders, baby 1, 2, 3.

Shoulders, hip, baby, 1, 2, 3.

Shoulders, hip, baby, 1, 2, 3.

Shoulders, hip, shoulders, hip,

Shoulders, hip, baby, 1, 2, 3.

Additional verses:

Hip, knees…

Knees, ankle…

Ankle, toes…

Toes, ankle…

Ankle, knees…

Knees, hips…

Hip, shoulders…

Shoulders, head…

Literacy Activities

(Select one or two follow-up activities to do each time you sing a song or say a rhyme.)

Oral Language Development

1. Most children learn to identify their body parts early. However, young children and children who speak English as a second language may still be working on getting all the names straight. Make sure all the children can identify the body parts named in the song.

THEME CONNECTIONS

Counting/Numbers

Parts of the Body

SEE ALSO

"I Can, You Can!" p. 153

"My Body Talks" p. 153

"My Hand on Myself" p. 152

"Say and Touch" p. 173

"Warm-Up Chant" p. 193

Phonological Awareness

1. Help the children identify the rhyming words, "toes" and "nose."

Learning Centers

Art (My Body)

Encourage the children to draw a self-portrait. With permission, help them label the body parts on their drawings.

Discovery (Eyewear)

Provide sunglasses, binoculars, magnifying glasses, and any other eyewear. Encourage the children to explore the different things we look through.

Dramatic Play (Hats Are for Heads)

Provide several different types of hats for children to explore, as well as a mirror. *What other things do we wear on our heads?*

Gross Motor (Knees Are Made for Crawling)

Use yarn to create a maze. Encourage the children to crawl through it. *Can you crawl without using your knees? Show me how you would do it.*

Outdoor Play or Music and Movement Activity

1. Teach the children to do shoulder rolls, knee bends, toe lifts, and if they are ready, head stands.
2. Sing along with "Head, Shoulders, Knees, and Toes" (*Where Is Thumbkin?* CD, Kimbo) or "I Like Me" (*I Am Special* CD, Thomas Moore).

BRAIN CONNECTIONS

This is a good exercise song. The brain needs oxygen, and exercising is one sure way to obtain it.

REFLECTIONS

Name some things you do with your head. What about your knees?

How are your toes and your fingers alike? How are they different?

Hey! My Name Is Joe

Hey, My Name Is Joe!

Hey, my name is Joe!
I have a wife, one kid and I work in a button factory.
One day, my boss said, "Are you busy?"
I said, "No."
"Then turn a button with your right hand." (make a turning gesture with right hand)

Hey, my name is Joe!
I have a wife, two kids, and I work in a button factory.
One day, my boss said, "Are you busy?"
I said, "No."
"Then turn a button with your left hand." (make a turning gesture with left hand
    as you continue with the right hand)

(Continue adding number of children and adding right and left feet and head.)

Hey, my name is Joe!
I have a wife, six kids, and I work in a button factory.
One day, my boss said, "Are you busy?"
I said, "Yes!"

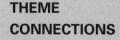

THEME CONNECTIONS

Community
Workers
Counting/Numbers
Emotions
Families
Humor
Movement

Related Songs, Chants, and Rhymes

Family Fun by Pam Schiller

Mommy and me dance and sing.
Daddy and me laugh and play.
Mommy, Daddy, and me
Dance and sing,
Laugh and play,
Kiss and hug,
A zillion times a day!

Johnny Works With One Hammer (Tune: Traditional)

Johnny works with one hammer,
One hammer, one hammer. (make hammering motion with right hand)
Johnny works with one hammer.
Then he works with two.

Johnny works with two hammers... (motion with left and right hands)
Johnny works with three hammers... (motion with both hands and right foot)
Johnny works with four hammers... (motion with both hands and both feet)
Johnny works with five hammers... (motion with both hands and feet and with head)
Then he goes to bed. (rest head on folded hands)

Literacy Activities

(Select one or two follow-up activities to do each time you sing a song or say a rhyme.)

Oral Language Development

1. Introduce words that may be new to the children, such as "factory," "button," and "boss."
2. Explain that Joe works in a button factory. Encourage the children to discuss the jobs of their family members.

Learning Centers

Fine Motor (Button Sort)

Provide a basket of buttons and encourage the children to sort them. Talk with them about their sorting criteria. *Did you sort by size? Color? Number of holes?*

SEE ALSO

"Catalina
   Magnalina"
   p. 35
"Miss Mary Mack"
   p. 143
"Ten in the Bed"
   p. 186

Games (Button Toss)

Place three or four squares of colored felt (or construction paper) on the floor. Use masking tape to make a play line on the floor about three feet away from the squares. Provide colored buttons that match the felt squares. Encourage the children to sit on the play line and toss buttons on the color square that matches the color of their button. Ask the children to describe where the buttons land.

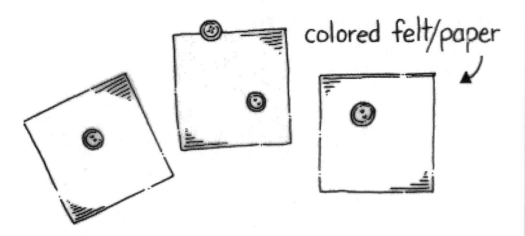

colored felt/paper

Gross Motor (Beanbag Walk)

Place a line of masking tape on the floor. Challenge the children to walk the line with a beanbag on their right shoulder. Next add a beanbag on the right shoulder and a beanbag on the head. Ask the children if the walk gets more difficult as beanbags are added.

Writing (My Name Is)

Cut pieces of tagboard into 4" x 18" strips. Print children's names on the strips, leaving enough space between the letters to draw puzzle lines. Laminate and cut into puzzle pieces. Provide a zipper-closure plastic bag for each child to use to store his or her name. Encourage the children to put their name puzzle together. Make a name puzzle for "Joe" and encourage the children to put it together.

Outdoor Play or Music and Movement Activity

1. Play Who's Got the Button? Have children sit in a circle. Choose a child to be IT and give IT a button. Ask the children to close their eyes. Help IT choose a friend to give the button to (secretly). Invite the children to open their eyes and try to guess who has the button. The child who guesses correctly becomes the next IT.
2. Sing along with "Family Dance" (*Thomas Moore Sings the Family* CD, Thomas Moore) or "Button Factory" (*Is Everybody Happy?* CD, Jean Feldman).

REFLECTIONS

What kind of work do you want to do when you grow up?

What kind of work does your mother or father do?

Hickory Dickory Dock

Hickory, Dickory, Dock

Hickory, dickory, dock
    (stand, swing arm like pendulum)
The mouse ran up the clock.
    (bend over; run hand up body)
The clock struck one,
    (clap hands over head once)
The mouse ran down.
    (run hand down to feet)
Hickory, dickory, dock.
    (stand, swing arm like pendulum)

**THEME
CONNECTIONS**

Animals

Houses and Homes

Movement

Nursery Rhymes

Opposites

Time of Day

SEE ALSO

"The Farmer in the
   Dell" p. 157
"Frog Went A-
   Courtin'"
   p. 70

Related Songs, Chants, and Rhymes

Old Gray Cat

The old gray cat is sleeping, sleeping, sleeping.
The old gray cat is sleeping in the house. (one child—the cat—curls up, pretending
   to sleep)
The little mice are creeping, creeping, creeping.
The little mice are creeping through the house. (other children—the mice—creep
   around the cat)
The old gray cat is waking, waking, waking.
The old gray cat is waking through the house. (cat slowly sits up and stretches)
The old gray cat is chasing, chasing, chasing.
The old gray cat is chasing through the house. (cat chases mice)
All the mice are squealing, squealing, squealing.
All the mice are squealing through the house. (mice squeal; when cat catches a
   mouse, that mouse becomes the cat)

Three White Mice (Tune: Three Blind Mice)

Three white mice, three white mice,
See how they dance, see how they dance.
They danced and danced for the farmer's wife,
Who played for them on a silver fife.
Did you ever see such a sight in your life,
As three white mice!

Literacy Activities

(Select one or two follow-up activities to do each time you sing a song or say a rhyme.)

Oral Language Development
1. Find out what the children know about mice. *Have you ever seen a mouse? Where did you see it? What was it doing? What color are mice?* Show photos, if available, to stimulate conversation.

Phonological Awareness
1. Point out the rhyming words ("dock" and "clock"). If you also teach "Three White Mice" (see Related Songs, Chants, and Rhymes), point out the rhyming words: "wife," "fife," and "life."

Learning Centers

Fine Motor (Glue the Tail on the Mice)
Show the children how to make thumbprint mice by pressing their thumbs into a stamp pad and making thumbprints on paper. Let them use a pen to add details. Provide one-inch pieces of thin yarn and encourage the children to glue the yarn tails on their fingerprint mice.

Gross Motor (Mice Maze)
Create a maze using chairs, blocks, boxes, and so on. Encourage the children to crawl through the maze pretending to be mice. Ask the children questions about mice in mazes. *Have you ever seen a mouse in a maze? How does it find its way through the maze?* Have the children try going through the maze a second time. *Is it easier the second time? Why?*

Science (Mice Up Close)
Fill the area with photos of mice. Provide magnifying glasses for children to get an up-close look. If a live mouse is available, adopt it for the day.

Writing (I Can Spell "Mice")
Write the word "mice" on several large index cards. Give the children glue in a squeeze bottle and encourage them to trace of the letters or make glue dots on the letter to create tactile letters. Talk with the children about Braille. Explain that blind people read by touching raised dots, which represent letters. After the glue dries, encourage the children to touch the letters with their eyes closed.

Outdoor Play or Music and Movement Activity

1. Play "Farmer in the Dell" (p. 157) with the children.
2. Sing along with "Hickory Dickory Dock" (*Sing to Learn With Dr. Jean* CD, Jean Feldman) or "Nursery Rhyme Medley" (*Walt Disney Records: Children's Favorite Songs Vol. 4* CD).

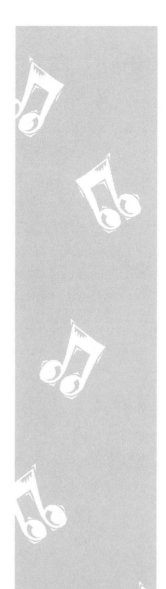

REFLECTIONS
Can you name some famous mice? (Mickey Mouse, Minnie Mouse, Jerry)

Do mice creep around? Why do people say they "creep"?

Home on the Range

Home on the Range
by Brewster Hegley (Tune: Traditional)

Oh, give me a home where the buffalo roam
Where the deer and the antelope play.
Where seldom is heard a discouraging word
And the skies are not cloudy all day.

Chorus:
Home, home on the range
Where the deer and the antelope play.
Where seldom is heard a discouraging word
And the skies are not cloudy all day.

How often at night when the heavens are bright
With the light from the glittering stars.
Have I stood there amazed and asked as I gazed
If their glory exceeds that of ours.

Chorus

Oh, I love those wild flow'rs in this dear land of ours
The curlew, I love to hear scream.
And I love the white rocks and the antelope flocks
That graze on the mountaintops green.

Chorus

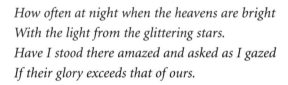

THEME CONNECTIONS

Animals

Cowboys and
   Cowgirls

Families

Houses and Homes

Way Out West

Related Songs, Chants, and Rhymes
Red River Valley (Tune: Traditional)

From this valley they say you are going.
I shall miss your blue eyes and sweet smile,
For you take with you all of the sunshine
That has brightened my pathway a while.
So consider a while ere you leave me,
Do not hasten to bid me adieu,

But remember the Red River Valley
And the cowboy who loved you so true.
As you go to your home by the ocean,
May you never forget those sweet hours
That we spent in the Red River Valley
And the love we exchanged in its bowers.

Buffalo Gals (Tune: Traditional)

As I was walking down the street,
Down the street, down the street,
A pretty little gal I chanced to meet.
Oh, she was fair to see.

Chorus

Buffalo Gals, won't you come out tonight,
Come out tonight, come out tonight.
Buffalo Gals, won't you come out tonight
And dance by the light of the moon.

I stopped her and we had a talk,
Had a talk, had a talk.
Her feet took up the whole sidewalk,
And left no room for me.

Chorus

I asked her if she'd have a dance,
Have a dance, have a dance.
I thought that I might have a chance
To shake a foot with her.

Chorus

I danced with a gal with a hole in her
stockin',
And her heel kept a-knockin', and her
toes kept a-rockin'.
I danced with a gal with a hole in her
stockin'
And we danced by the light of the moon.

Chorus

SEE ALSO
"Dusty" p. 121
"I'm a Texas Star"
p. 121
"Trigger" p. 122

Literacy Activities

(Select one or two follow-up activities to do each time you sing a song or say a rhyme.)

Oral Language Development

1. Discuss life out on the range. What does "range" mean? What does the range look like? Talk about descriptive words that are used in the song. If you have any pictures of wide open spaces show them to the children.

2. Discuss the concept of home. Ask the children what they think of when they think of home. Ask the children if they have ever heard of the phrase "Home Sweet Home." *What does it mean? Does home have to be a place? Might home just be any place that is comfortable? Ask the children if they have heard the phrase, "Home is where the heart is." What does it mean?*

3. Define the words that may be new to the children, such as "roam," "discouraging," "antelope," "glittering," "gaze," "curlew," and "flock."

Phonological Awareness

1. Help children identify the set of rhyming words in the chorus (play/day). Write the words on a chart and have the children brainstorm other words that rhyme with play and day.

Letter Knowledge and Recognition

1. Write the word "deer" on a piece of chart paper. Talk about deer. What do deer look like? What do they eat? How do they move? How are they different from

antelope? Write the word "dear" on the same piece of paper. Talk about the word "dear." What does it mean? How is it used? Ask the children, "what is the same" about the words (they sound alike) and what is different about the words (how they are spelled and what they mean). Ask them to look at both words and tell you which letters are the same. Which letter is different? Point out that the way we know the difference between the two words when they are spoken is in the way they are used. When the words are written we can tell the difference by noting the one letter that is different.

Learning Centers

Art (Range Pictures)
Provide tempera paint and large easel paper. Suggest the children paint pictures of "the range." Be sure to provide green, blue, white and brown paint. As the children paint, ask them to think about words in the song that describe what the range looks like. *What is said about the sky? What animals are mentioned? What color are the mountaintops? What color are the rocks?*

Blocks (Home on the Range)
Provide plastic animals, white rocks, and green and blue sheets of bulletin board paper. Challenge the children to create an open range.

Language (Home Is Where the Heart Is)
Give each child a heart-shaped piece of paper. Have them draw a place they feel at home. Ask the children to describe their home to you. With permission, transcribe their descriptions on the back of their heart drawing.

Writing (Home Sweet Home)
Encourage the children to write the words "Home Sweet Home" using magnetic letters. Write the words on chart paper or the chalkboard for them to use as a model. Discuss the words. *Which words are the same? Which word is different?*

Outdoor Play or Music and Movement Activity

1. Talk about how deer and antelope run and how they might play. Point out that both deer and antelope can leap high. Place a barrier of soft blocks in a safe spot and encourage the children to leap over the barrier like deer and antelope.

REFLECTIONS
What things in the song make you know that the person singing it loves the range?

How is a range like a farm? How is it different from a farm?

Hop and Rags

Hop and Rags
(Tune: My Dog Rags)

I have a horse and her name is Hop.
She runs so fast that it's hard to stop.
Her tail swish swashes, and her feet clip clop.
And when she runs she clip, clip clops!
Swish swash, plip plop, clip clop.
Swish swash, plip plop, clip clop.

My horse Hop she loves to neigh.
She neighs and neighs in the fields all day.
I say, "Hey you, come eat some hay."
But all she says is neigh, neigh, neigh.
Swish swash, clip clop, neigh neigh.
Swish swash, clip clop, neigh neigh.

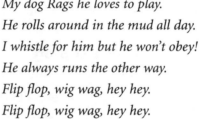

I have a dog and his name is Rags.
He eats so much that his tummy sags.
His ears flip flop and his tail wig wags,
And when he walks he zig, zig, zags!
Flip flop, wig wag, zig zag.
Flip flop, wig wag, zig zag.

My dog Rags he loves to play.
He rolls around in the mud all day.
I whistle for him but he won't obey!
He always runs the other way.
Flip flop, wig wag, hey hey.
Flip flop, wig wag, hey hey.

Related Songs and Chants

Where, Oh, Where Has My Little Dog Gone? (Tune: Traditional)
Where, oh, where has my little dog gone?
Where, oh, where can he be?
With his ears cut short and his tail cut long,
Oh, where, oh, where can he be?

Whose Dog Are Thou? (Tune: Traditional)
Bow, wow, wow. (face partner and stomp three times)
Whose dog are thou? (point index finger on left and right hand of partner)
Little Tommy Tucker's dog. (hold hands out to side)
Bow, wow, wow. (face partner and stomp three times)

THEME CONNECTIONS
Animals
Emotions
Pets

SEE ALSO
"Bingo" p. 32
"Fido" p. 32
"My Dog Rags"
   p. 33

Literacy Activities

(Select one of the follow-up activities to do each time you sing a song or say a rhyme.)

Oral Language Development

1. Discuss pets. Who has a pet? What is your pet's name? Where did your pet come from? On a piece of paper, write the types of pets that children mention. Which pets do the children have that are the same as those mentioned in the song?
2. If photos of pets are available, use them to stimulate discussion about different animals.
3. Teach the children the American Sign Language signs (appendix p. 239-241) for horse, dog, cat, rabbit, and parrot.

Print Awareness

1. Invite the children to brainstorm a list of all the songs they know about pets. Write the names of the songs on chart paper. After the list is made, group the list by type of pet. *How many songs do the children know about dogs? Fish? Horses? Cats?*

Learning Centers

Blocks (A Home of His Own)

Encourage the children to build a doghouse for a new puppy. Provide medium-sized cardboard boxes, tempera paint, and props such as dog pillows, bowls, and so on.

Dramatic Play (Pet Store)

Turn the center into a pet store. Add props such as pet supplies (collars, bowls, leashes, fish bowls, and so on). Put stuffed animals in pretend cages. Place "For Sale" signs on some of the cages. Encourage children to make "For Sale" signs for other cages.

Gross Motor (Dog Bowl Toss)

Use masking tape to create a throw line. Encourage the children to toss beanbags into a dog bowl. As children get more proficient, move the bowl further from the throw line.

Writing (Pets)

Write the names of all the pets mentioned in the song ("dog," "goldfish," "parrot," "bunny," "kitty," and so on) on index cards. Encourage the children to copy the names using tracing paper and crayons. Some children will be able to write the words. Suggest that they write the words on index cards and add them to their Word Box (shoebox collection of words they can write).

Outdoor Play or Music and Movement Activity

1. Play Dog and Bone. Ask the children to sit in a circle. Select one child to be IT. IT walks around the outside of the circle, carrying a paper or plastic bone. Eventually IT drops the bone behind a player. That player picks up the bone and chases IT around the circle. If he taps IT before they get around the circle, IT goes to the "doghouse" (center of the circle). If he doesn't, IT takes his place in the circle. The player with the bone becomes the new IT.

2. Sing along with "Where, Oh, Where Has My Little Dog Gone?" (*Here Is Thumbkin!* CD, Kimbo).

REFLECTIONS

Where else can you get a dog other than a pet store?

How do you take care of a pet?

Humpty Dumpty

Humpty Dumpty

Humpty Dumpty sat on a wall.
Humpty Dumpty had a great fall.
All the king's horses and all the king's men
Couldn't put Humpty together again.

Related Songs, Chants, and Rhymes

Humpty Dumpty Dumpty*

Everybody likes to Humpty
  Dumpty Dumpty.
Everybody likes to Humpty Dumpty
  Dumpty.
Oh, Humpty Dumpty sat on the wall.
Humpty Dumpty had a great fall.
Humpty Dumpty Dumpty.

All the boys like to Humpty Dumpty
  Dumpty.
All the boys like to Humpty Dumpty
  Dumpty.
Oh, Humpty Dumpty sat on the wall.
Humpty Dumpty had a great fall.
Humpty Dumpty Dumpty.

All the girls like to Humpty Dumpty
  Dumpty.
All the girls like to Humpty Dumpty
  Dumpty.
Oh, Humpty Dumpty sat on the wall.
Humpty Dumpty had a great fall.
Humpty Dumpty Dumpty.

Everybody likes to Humpty Dumpty
  Dumpty.
Everybody likes to Humpty Dumpty
  Dumpty.
Oh, Humpty Dumpty sat on the wall.
Humpty Dumpty had a great fall.
Humpty Dumpty Dumpty.

* From *I Am Special Just Because I'm Me* CD by Thomas Moore

Humpty Dumpty's New Ears by Pam Schiller

Humpty Dumpty sat on a wall.
Humpty Dumpty had a great fall.
All the king's horses and all the king's men
Couldn't put Humpty Dumpty together again.

THEME CONNECTIONS

Animals
Counting/Numbers
Humor
Kings and Queens
Nursery Rhymes
Parts of the Body
Problem Solving

Humpty Dumpty started to cry.
Humpty said, "Oh, please won't you try?"
His friend, Jack Horner, knew what to do.
He fixed Humpty Dumpty with his glue.

When Humpty Dumpty saw himself new,
He no longer felt all sad and blue,
He looked in the mirror and said with glee,
"Let's glue some ears to the side of me."

A pair of ears will look real nice,
Like they do on elephants and mice.
One on the left, and one on the right,
Humpty with ears—what a sight!

Jack made two ears and then with his glue
He carefully attached ear one, then ear two.
Humpty looked in the mirror and said
   with glee,
"I'm a good-looking egg, don't you agree?"

SEE ALSO
"The Grand Old
   Duke of York"
   p. 81
"Itsy Bitsy Spider"
   p. 130
"Nursery Rhyme
   Rap" p. 14
"There's a Hole in
   the Bucket"
   p. 189

Literacy Activities

(Select one or two follow-up activities to do each time you sing a song or say a rhyme.)

Oral Language Development

1. Discuss the original rhyme with the children. Ask questions about what the children think about the king's men giving up. *What could they have done instead? How would you have helped Humpty Dumpty?* Share one of the other versions ("Humpty Dumpty Dumpty" or "Humpty Dumpty's New Ears") with the children. *Which version of the rhyme do you like best?* Have the children brainstorm ways to fix the broken egg. Make a list of their suggestions.

Phonological Awareness

1. Point out the rhyming word relationship between Humpty's first and last name.

Letter Knowledge and Recognition

1. Write "Humpty Dumpty" on chart paper. Read it several times to the children. Ask them to identify the letters in the words that are the same and the ones that are different. Reinforce the idea that changing the first letter changes the word. Mention that changing one letter also creates a rhyming word relationship between the two words.

Learning Centers

Blocks (Humpty Dumpty Wall)

Suggest that the children build a wall with blocks. Provide plastic eggs and suggest that the children balance the eggs on the wall. *Is it easy to balance an egg? Why? Why not?*

Games (Egg Races)

Use masking tape to create a start line and finish line on the floor about 3' apart. Use two different colors of plastic tape to make travel lines between the start and finish line. Give the children plastic eggs to match the travel line and invite them to race their eggs along the line from the start line to the finish line. If the eggs fall off the line, the children must start over. The first egg to arrive at the finish line wins. Which children try to roll the egg end over end? Which roll the egg sideways? *Which way works best?*

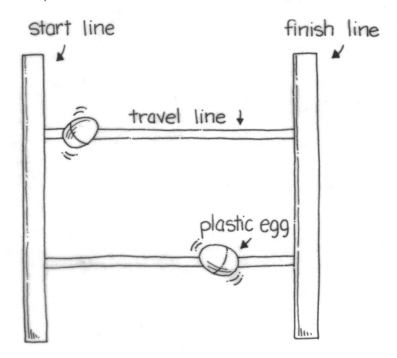

Language (Humpty Dumpty's Ears)

Encourage the children to retell the story of "Humpty Dumpty's New Ears." Ask them if they can think of anything else Humpty Dumpty might want now that he has found out about glue. (Hair?)

Writing (Humpty Dumpty)

Write "Humpty Dumpty" on chart paper. Encourage the children to use magnetic letters to copy Humpty Dumpty's name.

Outdoor Play or Music and Movement Activity

1. Teach the children how to do Humpty Dumpty Rolls (forward rolls). Make sure the surface the children are rolling on is soft (a rug, mat, or grass). Point out how much easier they can roll when they pull in their arms and legs tightly. *Why are these rolls called "Humpty Dumpty" rolls? What shape is your body when rolling?*

2. Sing and dance to "Humpty Dumpty Dumpty" (*I Am Special* CD, Thomas Moore). Sing along to "Nursery Rhyme Medley" (*Walt Disney Records: Children's Favorite Songs Vol. 3* CD).

BRAIN CONNECTIONS

Eggs are a good source of protein and, therefore, are good for the brain.

REFLECTIONS

Why is it important to try to fix broken things?

What do you think made Humpty Dumpty fall?

Hush, Little Baby

Hush, Little Baby
(Tune: Traditional)

Hush, little baby, don't say a word.
Mamma's gonna show you a mockingb
If that mockingbird won't sing,
Mamma's gonna show you a
    diamond ring.
If that diamond ring turns brass,
Mamma's gonna show you a
    looking glass.
If that looking glass gets broke,
Mamma's gonna show you a
    billy goat.
If that billy goat won't pull,
Mamma's gonna find you a cart
    and bull.
If that cart and bull turns over,
Mamma's gonna bring you a dog named Rover.
If that dog named Rover won't bark,
Mamma's gonna find you a horse and cart.
If that horse and cart fall down,
You'll still be the sweetest little baby in town.

(This song has been adapted to get away from the concept of buying things.)

Related Songs, Chants, and Rhymes

Rockabye, Baby (Tune: Traditional)

Rockabye, baby, in the tree top
When the wind blows, the cradle will rock.
When the bough breaks, the cradle will fall,
And down will come baby, cradle and all.

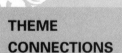

**THEME
CONNECTIONS**
Animals
Babies
Boats and Ships
Counting/Numbers
Families
Lullabies
Naptime/Sleeping
Rivers
Sun, Moon, Stars
Things That Go
    Together
Time of Day

SEE ALSO

"Are You Sleeping?"
p. 26
"Family Fun" p. 94
"Lazy Mary" p. 26

Wynken, Blynken, and Nod by Eugene Field

Wynken, Blynken, and Nod one night
Sailed off in a wooden shoe
Sailed on a river of crystal light,
Into a sea of dew.
"Where are you going, and what do you
wish?"
The old moon asked the three.
"We have come to fish for the herring fish
That live in this beautiful sea.
Nets of silver and gold have we!"
Said Wynken, Blynken, and Nod.

The old moon laughed and sang a song,
As they rocked in the wooden shoe,
And the wind that sped them all night
long,
Ruffled the waves of dew.
The little stars were the herring fish
That lived in that beautiful sea.
"Now cast your nets wherever you
wish—
Never afeared are we."
So cried the stars to the fishermen three:
Wynken, Blynken, and Nod.

All night long their nets they threw
To the stars in the twinkling foam;
Then down from the skies came the
wooden shoe,
Bringing the fishermen home.
'Twas all so pretty a sail it seemed
As if it could not be,
And some folks thought 'twas a dream
they'd dreamed
Of sailing that beautiful sea;
But I shall name you the fishermen three:
Wynken, Blynken, and Nod.

Wynken and Blynken are two little eyes
And Nod is a little head;
And the wooden shoe that sailed the skies
Is a wee one's trundle-bed.
So shut your eyes while mother sings
Of wonderful sights that be,
And you shall see the beautiful things
As you rock in the misty sea,
Where the old shoe rocked the fishermen
three:
Wynken, Blynken, and Nod.

Literacy Activities

(Select one or two follow-up activities to do each time you sing a song or say a rhyme.)

Oral Language Development

1. Define the words in the song that may be new vocabulary for the children, such as "mockingbird," "looking glass," "brass," and "cart." Explain that "Hush, Little Baby" is a lullaby. (You may need to define lullaby.)

2. Tell the children (older children) that in one of the original forms of the song, the word "buy" is used instead of "show." Ask the children about things a mother might show her baby to calm him or her. Make a list of their responses. Lead the children to understand that buying something for someone is not necessary when there are so many beautiful and interesting things readily available at no cost to enjoy (e.g., flowers, sunrise, animals, music, and so on). Remind them that babies love to stare at new and interesting sights.

3. Teach the children the American Sign Language sign (appendix p. 239-240) for baby, mother, and father.

Phonological Awareness

1. Write the words to "Hush, Little Baby" on chart paper. As you sing the song, point to the words on the paper.

Learning Centers

Dramatic Play (Nursery)

Add nursery props (dolls, rocking chair, lullaby tapes, baby bed, storybooks, and so forth) to the center. Encourage the children to role-play putting the baby to bed.

Fine Motor (Bring Back the Shine)

Give children some brass polish and some pieces of brass to polish. Talk with them while they work about things that are made out of brass, such as figurines, pots, jewelry, eating utensils, and so forth.

Caution: Supervise this activity closely to make sure children do not breathe in the fumes, eat any of it, or get any in their eyes. You may wish to have them pretend to use brass polish to polish the brass pieces instead.

Language (Hush Little Baby)

Encourage the children to sing the song using the chart paper with the words on it. If desired, prepare sentence strips and let the children use them and then illustrate them.

Listening (Lullabies)

Play lullaby tapes for the children to enjoy. Add some books for them to look at while they listen.

Outdoor Play or Music and Movement Activity

1. Play Possum. Ask the children to lie very still and pretend to be asleep while lullaby music plays. When the music stops, they get up from their sleeping spot and run to another spot and get into a sleeping position. When the music starts again they can't move. If they do move while they are pretending to sleep, they are out of the game.
2. Play songs from Thomas Moore's *Sleepy Time* CD. Sing along to "Hush Little Baby" (*Here Is Thumbkin!* CD).

BRAIN CONNECTIONS
Sleep is important for good brain care. While we sleep our brain is able to file away all the things we have learned during the day and get ready for new things we will learn tomorrow.

REFLECTIONS
Of all the things mentioned in the song, which thing would you like best? Why?

Does anyone sing you a lullaby to help you fall asleep? If yes, who? If no, would you like to hear a song as you go to sleep? Perhaps you might ask your mother or father to sing you a lullaby. Or maybe you could sing one for them.

I Dropped My Dolly in the Dirt

I Dropped My Dolly in the Dirt

(Tune: A Sailor Went to Sea)

I dropped my dolly in the dirt,
I asked my dolly if it hurt.
But all my dolly said to me,
"Whaa! Whaa! Whaa!"

Related Songs, Chants, and Rhymes

Floppy Rag Doll

(suit actions to words)
Flop your arms, flop your feet,
Let your hand go free.
You're the floppiest rag doll
I am ever going to see.

Say, Say, My Playmate (Tune: Traditional)

Say, say, my playmate,
Come out and play with me,
And bring your dollies three.
Climb up my apple tree.

Look down my rain barrel.
Slide down my cellar door,
And we'll be jolly friends
Forever more, 1-2-3-4.

Literacy Activities

(Select one or two follow-up activities to do each time you sing a song or say a rhyme.)

Oral Language Development

1. Discuss dolls. *Where do you buy dolls? Who plays with dolls? How many kinds of dolls are there?* Explain that boys and girls play with dolls. Help them understand that the super-hero figures, movie-action figures, and small plastic characters are all dolls.

THEME CONNECTIONS

Emotions
Friends
Movement
Parts of the Body
Things I Like/
    Favorite Things

Phonological Awareness

1. Call attention to the crying sound of the doll. "Whaa!" is a word that sounds like the sound it is describing. It is an example of **onomatopoeia**.

Letter Knowledge and Recognition

1. Write the words "doll" and "dolly" on chart paper or with magnetic letters on a magnetic board. Ask the children which letters in the words are the same. Which letter is different? Point out that to change the word "doll" to "dolly," a "y" has to be added at the end.

Learning Centers

Art (Dirty Dolls)

Cut out large paper dolls from easel paper or construction paper. Give the children sponges and brown tempera paint. Encourage the children to sponge paint the dolls to look like they have been dropped in the dirt.

Blocks (Small Dolls)

Provide small action and/or movie figures or plastic characters. Remind the children that some dolls are small and are sold in the different sections of the toy store.

Construction (Dolls Made of Clay)

Encourage the children to shape dolls from clay or playdough. Provide yarn, buttons, wiggle eyes, scraps of fabric, and other decorative items.

Writing (I Can Spell "Dolly")

Write the words "doll" and "dolly" on index cards. Encourage the children to spell both words with magnetic letters. *How do you change the word "doll" to "dolly"?*

Outdoor Play or Music and Movement Activity

1. Play some music and encourage the children to pretend to be floppy rag dolls. Extend the activities by turning it into a game of Freeze. Tell the children that when the music stops, they must freeze in the position they are in and be as still as statues.
2. Try some of these music and movement ideas:
   - Demonstrate how a wind-up doll might move and encourage the children to pretend to be wind-up dolls.
   - Sing along to "Say, Say, My Playmate" (*Thinkable, Movable, Lovable Songs* CD, ProVideo Productions).

REFLECTIONS

Have you ever fallen in the dirt? Why did you fall? What did you do when you fell? Did you get hurt?

What kind of dolls do you have at home? Where did your dolls come from? Do you play with them? Do you sleep with them?

Do you think that only girls play with dolls? What are the super hero and movie character figurines? Are they dolls?

I Know "Flea Fly Flow Mosquito"

Flea Fly Flow Mosquito

Flea fly
Flea fly flow
Flea fly flow mosquito
Oh no-no, no more mosquitoes
Itchy itchy scratchy scratchy, ooh I got one down my backy!
Eet biddly oatten boatten boe boe boe ditten dotten
Wye doan choo oo

Chase that
Big bad bug
Make it go away!
SHOO! SHOO!

Related Songs, Chants, and Rhymes

A Flea and a Fly

A flea and a fly
Flew up in a flue.
Said the flea, "Let us fly!"
Said the fly, "Let us flee!"
So they flew through a flap in the flue.

Shoo Fly (Tune: Traditional)

Shoo fly, don't bother me, (walk in a circle to the left)
Shoo fly, don't bother me, (walk in a circle to the left)
Shoo fly, don't bother me, (walk in a circle to the left)
I don't want to play today. (place hands on hips and shake head "no")

Flies in the buttermilk (walk around shooing flies)
Shoo fly, shoo.
Flies in the buttermilk
Shoo fly, shoo.

THEME CONNECTIONS

Animals
Humor
Insects

Flies in the buttermilk
Shoo fly, shoo.
Please just go away. (place hands on hips and shake head "no")

Shoo fly, don't bother me, (walk in a circle to the left)
Shoo fly, don't bother me, (walk in a circle to the left)
Shoo fly, don't bother me, (walk in a circle to the left)
Come back again another day. (wave good-bye)

Mosquitoes by Pam Schiller (Tune: Mary Had a Little Lamb)

Mosquitoes like it wet and damp,
Wet and damp, wet and damp.
Mosquitoes like it wet and damp,
They hang out where you camp.

Mosquitoes fly around in swarms
Around in swarms, around in swarms.
Mosquitoes fly around in swarms.
They have wings for arms.

Mosquitoes bite your arms and face
Arms and face, arms and face.
Mosquitoes bite your arms and face,
They like the way you taste.

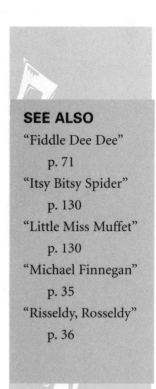

SEE ALSO
"Fiddle Dee Dee"
p. 71
"Itsy Bitsy Spider"
p. 130
"Little Miss Muffet"
p. 130
"Michael Finnegan"
p. 35
"Risseldy, Rosseldy"
p. 36

Literacy Activities

(Select one or two follow-up activities to do each time you sing a song or say a rhyme.)

Oral Language Development

1. Discuss bugs that bite or sting like fleas and mosquitoes. Encourage the children to tell about their experiences with biting bugs.

Comprehension

1. Ask the children questions about the nonsense words in the song. *What does "flea fly flow" mean? What does "Eet biddly oatten boatten boe boe boe ditten dotten" mean?* Explain that nonsense words often appear in songs and chants just to create an interesting rhythm or rhyme. Can the children think of another song with nonsense words in it? ("Willowby Wallaby" or "Ram Sam Sam")

Phonological Awareness

1. Help the children identify the alliteration in the song (flea fly flow/ boatten boe boe boe/ ditten dotten/big bad bug. Remind the children that repetition of sounds at the beginning of words in a row is called **alliteration.**

Print Awareness

1. Write the song on chart paper and sing it while pointing to the words. Call attention to the left-to-right and top-to-bottom progression of the text.

Letter Knowledge and Recognition

1. Print the words "Flea Fly Flow" on chart paper. Ask the children to identify the letters they recognize. *Which letters appear in each word? What letter is the first letter in each word?* Remind the children that the repetitive letter in the beginning of each word is called alliteration.

Learning Centers

Fine Motor (Mosquito Mouthpiece)

Give the children a small cup of water and a large eyedropper to represent a mosquito's mouthpiece. Have the children use the mouthpiece to suck up the water and put it in an empty cup. How long does it take to empty the glass?

Math (Counting Insect Body Parts)

Give the children pictures or photographs of a flea, a fly, and a mosquito. Have them count the legs, body parts, and antennae of each insect. Does each insect have the same number of legs? Body parts? Antennae?

Science (Insects)

Place photographs of insects in the science center. Have the children sort the photos by those that bite or sting and those that don't bite or sting.

Writing (Flea Fly Flow)

Print "Flea," "Fly," and "Flow" on chart paper. Encourage the children to copy the words with magnetic letters. Talk with them as they work. Point out that the first letter in each word is an "F".

Outdoor Play or Music and Movement Activity

1. Invite the children to play "Shoo Fly" (See Related Songs, Chants, and Rhymes).
2. Play some "hopping and flying" music and invite the children to hop like fleas and fly like flies and mosquitoes.

REFLECTIONS

How are mosquitoes and flies alike? How are they different?

Which part of the song is the silliest? Why?

I Love the Mountains

I Love the Mountains

(Tune: Traditional)

I love the mountains.
I love the rolling hills.
I love the flowers.
I love the daffodils.

Boom-de-otta, boom-de-otta,
Boom-de-otta, boom-de-otta. Boom!

Related Songs, Chants, and Rhymes

America the Beautiful by Katharine Lee Bates (Tune: Traditional)

Oh beautiful for spacious skies,
For amber waves of grain,
For purple mountain majesties
Above thy fruited plain!

Oh beautiful for pilgrim feet,
Whose stern, impassioned stress,
A thoroughfare for freedom beat,
Across the wilderness.

America! America! God shed his
*   grace on thee,*
And crown thy good with brotherhood,
From sea to shining sea!

America! America! God mend
*   thine every flaw,*
Confirm thy soul in self control,
Thy liberty in law.

The Ash Grove (Tune: Traditional)

Down yonder green valley, where streamlets meander
Where twilight is fading, I pensively roam.
Or at the bright noontide in solitude wander
Amidst the dark shades of the lonely ash grove.
'Tis there where the blackbird is cheerfully singing
Each warbler enchants with his notes from a tree.
Ah, then little think I of sorrow or sadness
The ash grove enchanting spells beauty for me.

THEME CONNECTIONS

Caring for Our
    World/Ecology
Colors
Holidays/Celebrations
Oceans
Patriotism
Nature
Sounds of Language
Things I Like/
    Favorite Things

The Earth Is My Home by Beverly Irby (Tune: The Farmer in the Dell)

Earth is our home.

Earth is our home.

For people and for animals

Earth is our home.

Let's keep our home clean.

Let's keep our home clean.

For people and for animals,

Let's keep our home clean.

(Repeat first verse.)

I Love the Ocean by Pam Schiller

I love the ocean

I love the sandy shore,

I love the seashells

Rolling on the ocean floor.

I love the sight of gulls in the sky

I love the sound of waves rushing by.

I love the pattern of shells on the beach

And little sea creatures just out of my reach.

I love the taste of salt in the air

I love the feel of nary a care,

I love the thought of sand in my hair

Tangled and wet—I really don't care.

I love the ocean from sunrise to sunset

I make lots of memories I'll never forget.

Literacy Activities

(Select one or two follow-up activities to do each time you sing a song or say a rhyme.)

Oral Language Development

1. Discuss the difference between mountains and hills. *Which are bigger? What are rolling hills?*

2. If available, show the children pictures of beautiful things in nature, such as trees, mountains, fields of flowers, lightening storms, and so forth. Use the photos to stimulate conversation about what they think are beautiful things in nature.

3. Teach the children the American Sign Language sign (appendix p. 239-241) for mountains, hills, flowers, and love. Try singing the song and using the signs at the same time.

4. Invite the children to sing the song, substituting "like" for "love." Try substituting "see" for "love." *Does changing a word change the impact of the song?* Can the children think of another word to substitute?

Print Awareness

1. Write the word "love" on chart paper. Ask children to name some things that they love. Make a list of their responses and read the list out loud when you are finished.

Learning Centers

Blocks (Rolling Hills)

Paint an old sheet with brown, green, and gray spray paint to create terrain. Encourage the children to stuff old towels under the terrain to create hills. Provide props such as trees and flowers to decorate the hills. Encourage the children to build homes out of blocks on the land.

Discovery (Nature Observation)

Make a nature observation bottle by putting nature items such as acorns, leaves, bits of moss, shells, rocks, and flowers in a clear plastic one-liter bottle.

Fine Motor (Nature's Gifts)

Provide several magazines with pictures of mountains, trees, flowers, and other beautiful things in nature. Encourage the children to cut out the pictures of things they like and create a collage of "Nature's Gifts." Ask questions about their choices. *Why did you choose this picture? Which thing is your favorite?*

Writing (What Do You Love?)

Encourage the children to describe something that they love. Transcribe their thoughts onto a sheet of paper and invite them to illustrate their responses.

Outdoor Play or Music and Movement Activity

1. Take the children on a nature walk. Make a list of things you think you will see before you leave. When you return check off the items that you actually saw. Place a piece of masking tape (sticky side out) around the wrist of each child. Encourage them to pick up nature items they like and stick them to the tape to create a Nature Bracelet.

2. Sing along to "This Land Is My Land" (*Esté es mí tierra* CD, José Lluis Orozco Productions).

REFLECTIONS

What are some things in nature that you really like?

What thing did you describe and write about today?

How can we take care of the Earth?

I Wish I Were

I Wish I Were
(Tune: If You're Happy and You Know It)

Oh, I wish I were a little juicy orange, juicy orange.
Oh, I wish I were a little juicy orange, juicy orange.
I'd go squirty, squirty, squirty
Over everybody's shirty.
Oh, I wish I were a little juicy orange, juicy orange.

Oh, I wish I were a little bar of soap, bar of soap.
Oh, I wish I were a little bar of soap, bar of soap.
I'd go slidy, slidy, slidy
Over everybody's body.
Oh, I wish I were a little bar of soap, bar of soap.

Oh, I wish I were a little blob of mud, blob of mud.
Oh, I wish I were a little blob of mud, blob of mud.
I'd go gooey, gooey, gooey
Over everybody's shoey.
Oh, I wish I were a little blob of mud, blob of mud.

Oh, I wish I were a little cookie crumb, cookie crumb.
Oh, I wish I were a little cookie crumb, cookie crumb.
I'd go crumby, crumby, crumby
Over everybody's tummy.
Oh, I wish I were a little cookie crumb, cookie crumb.

Oh, I wish I were a little radio, radio.
Oh, I wish I were a little radio, radio.
I'd go CLICK!

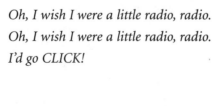

THEME CONNECTIONS
Animals
Humor
Real and Make-
    Believe
Things I Like/
    Favorite Things

118

Related Songs, Chants, and Rhymes

I Wish I Had a Dinosaur by Pam Schiller

I wish I had a dinosaur
That I could call my own,
I'd take him with me everywhere
He'd never be alone.

A football field would be his bed
A swimming pool his tub,
I'd need a ladder to reach his head
A blanket for a rub.

I'd need bushels of leafy food
A tree for playing fetch,
Bundles of cloth to make his clothes
And a basketball for catch.

I'd call him Dino De Dandee
He'd be my bestest friend.
When you saw him—you'd see me,
That's how close we would be.

I wish I had a dinosaur
To call my very own
I'd take him with me everywhere
I'd never be alone.

SEE ALSO
"Star Light, Star Bright" p. 211

Literacy Activities

(Select one or two follow-up activities to do each time you sing a song or say a rhyme.)

Oral Language Development

1. Invite the children to talk about things they wish for. You might pass a "magic pebble" or a "magic wand" around the circle and let each child make a wish. Mention to the children that most of the time, we must be responsible for making our wishes come true. For instance, we may have to work hard to get what we want. We might have to be patient and wait for something that we want. Sometimes we have to make a plan. Talk about something you wished for, perhaps a special trip or a new car. Outline how you helped make your wish come true.

2. Encourage the children to make a list of all the things that people use to make wishes, for example, a star, penny, birthday candle, and a wishbone.

Phonological Awareness

1. Help the children identify the rhyming words (squirty/shirty, gooey/shoey, and crummy/tummy). Discuss the nonsense words used to keep the song rhyming.

Learning Centers

Art (Squirty Masterpieces)

Fill squirt bottles with thinned orange paint. Encourage the children to squirt the paint onto butcher paper to create a "Squirty Masterpiece." Cover the floor with a drop cloth to protect from accidental over-shootings.

Discovery (Radio Investigation)

Place an old radio in the center and invite the children to explore finding a station. Discuss the function of the various knobs. Ask questions. *Do you listen to radios? Where? When?*

Language (Wish Making)

Fill the center with things (or photos of things) that we typically use for making wishes, such as a lucky penny, wishbone, star, birthday candle, and so forth. Talk with the children about wishes. *What really makes wishes come true? What stories can you remember hearing that had something about a wish in them?*

Writing (My Wish)

Invite the children to describe a special wish they have. Transcribe it onto a sheet of paper and encourage the children to illustrate their wish. Ask them what they might be able to do to make their wish come true.

Outdoor Play or Music and Movement Activity

1. Provide materials such as mud, pie tins, spoons, acorns, leaves, and sticks for the children to make mud pies. *Is the mud gooey?*
2. Sing along to "I Wish I Were" (*Dr. Jean Sings Silly Songs* CD, Jean Feldman).

REFLECTIONS

How do wishes come true?

Which verse of the song do you think is the funniest? Why?

I'm a Texas Star

I'm a Texas Star
(Tune: Turkey in the Straw)

I'm a Texas, I'm a Texas,
I'm a Texas star.
I come from the west where the cowboys/girls are
I can ride 'em, I can rope 'em
I can show 'em how it's done.
Come on (child's name), let's have some fun.

Related Songs, Chants, and Rhymes

Dusty (Tune: Bingo)

There was a cowboy
Who rode a horse
And Dusty was his name-o,
D-U-S-T-Y
D-U-S-T-Y
D-U-S-T-Y
And Dusty was his name-o.

Home on the Range by Brewster Hegley (Tune: Traditional)

Oh, give me a home where the buffalo roam,
Where the deer and the antelope play,
Where seldom is heard a discouraging word,
And the skies are not cloudy all day.

Chorus:
Home, home on the range
Where the deer and the antelope play,
Where seldom is heard a discouraging word,
And the skies are not cloudy all day.

THEME CONNECTIONS
Animals
Colors
Cowboys/Cowgirls
Nature
Sun, Moon, Stars
Way Out West

SEE ALSO

"Old MacDonald
Had a Farm"
p. 156

How often at night when the heavens are bright
With the light from the glittering stars,
Have I stood there amazed and asked as I gazed
If their glory exceeds that of ours.

Chorus

Oh, I love these wild flowers in this dear land of ours;
The curlew, I love to hear scream;
And I love the white rocks and the antelope flocks
That graze on the mountaintops green.

Chorus

Trigger by Richele Bartkowiak (Tune: Six Little Ducks)
My little horsie's name is Trigger
He ate so much he got bigger and bigger
His mouth chomp chomps
And his tail goes swish
And when he trots he clip-clap-clomps!

Chomp, chomp,
Swish, clip,
Clap, clomp!

Literacy Activities

(Select one or two follow-up activities to do each time you sing a song or say a rhyme.)

Oral Language Development
1. Find out what the children know about cowboys and cowgirls. *What clothing do they wear? What do they do? Has anyone been to a rodeo?* You will probably get a lot of television answers to your questions. Try to help children understand that cowboys and cowgirls serve a real purpose even today.
2. Define words that may be unfamiliar to the children ("Texas," "west," and "rope 'em").

Learning Centers

Blocks (Home at the Ranch)
Provide western props, including plastic horses and cows, small pieces of fabric for blankets, yarn rope, and so forth. Challenge the children to build a ranch. If pictures or photos are available, display them.

Discovery (Here Come the Horses)

Some children may have seen cowboys on television place their ears to the ground to determine if a horseback rider is coming. Explain that sound travels by vibrations. Have them place their hand on their throat and say their name as an example. Ask them to place their ear on a tabletop while you lightly tap on the opposite end of the table. This will allow them to feel and hear the sound vibrations. Explain that this is similar to the sound cowboys hear when they put their ear to the ground.

Gross Motor (Horseshoes)

Invite the children to play a game of horseshoes. Make mock horseshoes by cutting the center from plastic coffee can lids. Fill a 1/2-liter soda bottle with sand and use it as a stake. Encourage the children to toss the rings over the bottles from a few feet away. As they improve, have them increase the distance between the throw line and the stake.

Writing (I Can Spell "Texas")

Write the word "Texas" on an index card. Provide a tray of sand for the children and encourage them to use a stick to write "Texas" in the sand.

Outdoor Play or Music and Movement Activity

1. Teach the children how to gallop like horses.
2. Teach the children a Square Dance. Explain that square dancing is part of western culture. Have the children choose a partner. Arrange them in a square. You may want to make a masking tape square on the floor for the children to use. Invite them to follow these simple steps:
   - Bow to your partner. (*bow*)
   - Swing your partner. (*lock arms and spin around twice*)
   - Do-si-do. (*fold arms across chest and "back" around partner*)
   - Promenade. (*partners hold hands, right and left hands together, and walk around the square*)
3. Sing along to "Deep in the Heart of Texas" (*A Whole Lot of Animals* CD, Joel Reese), "Home on the Range" (*Rockin' Rhymes and Good Ol' Times* CD, Jean Feldman), or "Home on the Range" (*Walt Disney Records: Children's Favorite Songs Vol.1* CD).

REFLECTIONS

What new information did you learn about cowboys and cowgirls?

If you had a horse, what would you name it?

If You're Happy and You Know It

If You're Happy and You Know It
(Tune: Traditional)

If you're happy and you know it, clap your hands. (clap hands twice)
If you're happy and you know it, clap your hands. (clap hands twice)
If you're happy and you know it then your face will show it. (point to face)
If you're happy and you know it, clap your hands. (clap hands twice)

Other verses:
If you're happy and you know it, stomp your feet… (stomp feet twice)
If you're happy and you know it, shout "Hooray!"… (shout "hurray!")
If you're happy and you know it, do all three… (clap hands twice, stomp feet twice, and shout "hurray!")

Related Songs, Chants, and Rhymes

I Have Something in My Pocket (Tune: Traditional)

I have something in my pocket.
It belongs across my face.
I keep it very close at hand.
In a most convenient place.

I bet you could guess it,
If you guessed a long, long while
So I'll take it out and put it on,
It's a great big happy SMILE!

Literacy Activities

(Select one or two follow-up activities to do each time you sing a song or say a rhyme.)

Listening

1. Change the lyrics to the song. For example, you might say, "If you're happy and you know it, point to something red." Or "point to a friend," "rub your chin," and "pat your head." Make up your own things to do and let the children make suggestions, too.

Oral Language Development

1. Discuss the words in the song that may be new vocabulary for the children, such as "stomp," and "hooray."

THEME CONNECTIONS

Emotions
Humor
Movement
Parts of the Body
Self

2. Discuss other words for happy such as joyful, glad, blissful, pleased, and ecstatic. Clap out the syllables for the word "happy" and then choose one of the other words with the same number of syllables. Sing the song, inserting the new word.

Letter Knowledge and Recognition

1. Write the words "clap," "stomp," and "hooray" on large index cards. Show the children the cards and discuss the letters in each word. Sing the song again, mixing up the verses. Use the cards to indicate to the children which reaction to use for each verse. Be sure to compliment the children on being able to read directions so well. (For younger children, make picture clues on each card. Add a hand to the card for clapping, a foot to the card for stomping, and a mouth on the card for shouting hooray.) Save the cards to be used in the writing center.

Learning Centers

Fine Motor (Happy Face Collage)

Provide magazines and scissors. Encourage the children to cut out pictures of happy faces and glue them to a piece of paper to create a happy face collage. Encourage the children to think of things that might make the people in the pictures happy. Ask them to share their thoughts.

Language (What Makes Me Happy?)

Encourage the children to dictate sentences about what makes them happy. Transcribe their thoughts on drawing paper and encourage them to illustrate their ideas.

Math (Counting Claps and Stomps)

Provide numeral cards for the numbers one to five. Have the children clap the number of times indicated by each card. Ask questions. *Which card directs them to clap the most times? Which card directs them to clap the least number of times?*

SEE ALSO
"This Is Austin" p. 150
"This Little Light of Mine" p. 192
"Where Do You Wear Your Ears?" p. 49

Writing (Word Tracing)

Place index cards with the words "clap," "stomp," or "hooray" on them in the center along with tracing paper and pencils. Invite the children to trace the words on the tracing paper. Ask them to examine the letters they are tracing to see if any of the letters are the same letters they have in their name. Some children will be able to write the words. Suggest that they write the words on index cards and add them to their Word Box (shoebox collection of words they can write).

Outdoor Play or Music and Movement Activity

1. Provide chalk and encourage the children to draw happy faces on the sidewalk.
2. Have a Happy Day Parade. Invite the children to carry or wear something that makes them feel happy. Ask children to explain why the item makes them feel happy.
3. Invite the children to sing along with "If You're Happy and You Know It" (*Singing, Moving, and Learning* CD, Thomas Moore), "If You're Happy and You Know It" (*Where Is Thumbkin?* CD, Kimbo), "If You're Happy and You Know It" (*Is Everybody Happy?* CD, Jean Feldman), "If You're Happy and You Know It" (*Walt Disney Records: Children's Favorite Songs Vol. 3* CD), or "I Have Something in My Pocket" (*Thinkable, Movable, Lovable Songs* CD, ProVideo Productions).

BRAIN CONNECTIONS

Emotions boost memory. When we feel happy and content, our bodies increase the level of endorphins in our blood stream. Endorphins act as a memory fixative. Laughter also causes the release of endorphins. Feeling happy and laughing are both ways to increase our potential for remembering information and experiences.

REFLECTIONS

What makes you feel happy? Why?

What new verse would you add to "If You're Happy and You Know It?"

The Iguana in Lavender Socks

The Iguana in Lavender Socks
by Pam Schiller (Tune: On Top of Old Smokey)

On top of a hillside,
All covered with rocks,
There lives an iguana
With lavender socks.

She bathes in the sunshine
And cools in the lake.
She dines on tamales
And fly-covered cake.

When she is happy,
She plays her guitar,
And all the iguanas,
Think she's a rock star.

They dance on the hillside
And over the rocks.
They dance with the iguana
In lavender socks.

I love that iguana,
She's totally cool,
I wish that iguana
Would dance to my school.

THEME CONNECTIONS
Animals
Colors
Humor
Kings and Queens
Real and Make-
　　Believe
Reptiles
Things I Like/
　　Favorite Things
Work

Related Songs, Chants, and Rhymes

Lavender's Blue (Tune: Traditional)

Lavender's blue, dilly dilly,
Lavender's green,
When I am king, dilly dilly,
You shall be queen.
Call up your men, dilly, dilly,
Set them to work,

Some to the plough, dilly, dilly,
Some to the cart.
Some to make hay, dilly, dilly,
Some to cut corn,
While you and I, dilly, dilly,
Keep ourselves warm.

SEE ALSO

"There Once Was a Turtle" p. 205

"Tiny Tim" p. 205

Five Dancing Dinosaurs by Pam Schiller

Five huge dinosaurs dancing a jig. (hold up five fingers and dance them)

They rumble and grumble and stumble

Because they are so big. (spread hands apart)

Five huge dinosaurs floating on a barge. (hold up five fingers and make a boat with hands)

They jiggle and wiggle and jiggle

Because they are so large. (spread hands apart)

Five huge dinosaurs singing a song. (hold up five fingers and put hands beside mouth)

They bellow and holler and ramble

Because they sing it wrong. (shake head no)

Five huge dinosaurs taking a bow. (hold up five fingers and bow)

They bobble and hobble and tumble

Because they don't know how. (hold hands out to side)

Five huge dinosaurs making me laugh. (hold up five fingers and then hold tummy)

They stumble when they dance. (dance fingers on arm)

They jiggle when they float. (make boat with hands)

The ramble when they sing. (place hands beside mouth)

They tumble when they bow. (bow)

But they can make me laugh! (hold tummy, shake head "yes")

Literacy Activities

(Select one or two follow-up activities to do each time you sing a song or say a rhyme.)

Oral Language Development

1. Define words that may be new vocabulary for the children, for example, "iguana," "lavender," "rock star," and "totally cool."

2. Find out what the children know about iguanas. *Have you ever seen an iguana wearing socks? What do iguanas look like? What color are they?* Show the children a photograph of a real iguana, if available. Ask them what other animal the iguana looks like.

Phonological Awareness

1. Help the children identify the rhyming words (socks/rocks, lake/cake, guitar/star, and school/cool). Ask them to think of other words that rhyme with "socks" and "rocks."

Print Awareness

1. Write "The Iguana in Lavender Socks" on chart paper. Sing the song while pointing out the left to right and top to bottom progression of the print.

Learning Centers

Art (Lavender Paints)

Give the children lavender tempera paint and encourage them to paint a lavender picture. You may want to start with purple and white paint and let the children create lavender by mixing the two colors.

Dramatic Play (Totally Cool Iguanas)

Provide song props, including sunglasses, a toy guitar, and lavender socks. Encourage the children to pretend to be "totally cool iguanas."

Science (Observation and Exploration)

Place photos of real iguanas in the center for children to observe details. Also place a variety of rocks in the center for children to explore.

Writing (I Can Spell "Iguana")

Give the children magnetic letters and encourage them to spell "iguana." Provide a model for them to copy. Some children will be able to write the word. Suggest that they write the word on an index card and add it to their Word Box (shoebox collection of words they can write).

Outdoor Play or Music and Movement Activity

1. In advance of this lesson, collect old pairs of socks from families. Dye the socks lavender. Provide a pair of socks for each child and encourage them to dance in lavender socks. *Does dancing in lavender socks feel any different than dancing without them?*

BRAIN CONNECTIONS

Both the color and the aroma of lavender have a calming effect on the brain. Keep lavender hand lotion by the sink and encourage the children to use it when they wash their hands after lunch. It will help them calm down for naptime.

REFLECTIONS

What would you think if an iguana wearing lavender socks danced into our school?

Do you think real iguanas dance?

Itsy Bitsy Spider

Itsy Bitsy Spider

(Tune: Traditional)

The itsy bitsy spider
Went up the water spout.
Down came the rain
And washed the spider out.
Out came the sun
And dried up all the rain.
And the itsy bitsy spider
Went up the spout again.

Related Songs, Chants, and Rhymes

Little Miss Muffet

Little Miss Muffet sat on her tuffet,
Eating her curds and whey.
Along came a spider,
And sat down beside her,
And frightened Miss Muffet away.

(Optional additional verse by Tamera Bryant and Pam Schiller)
Little Miss Muffet went back to her tuffet,
Looked the thing square in the eye.
"See here, you big spider,
Miss Muffet's a fighter
And you're the one saying 'bye-bye.'"

THEME CONNECTIONS

Emotions

Food

Insects

Nursery Rhymes

Spatial
   Relationships

Sun, Moon, Stars

Weather

Literacy Activities

(Select one or two follow-up activities to do each time you sing a song or say a rhyme.)

Oral Language Development

1. Discuss some of the words that may be new vocabulary for the children, such as "itsy bitsy," "water spout," and so on. Ask the children to provide examples of things that go up and down (an elevator, airplane, escalator, pulley, blind). *What things on your body can go up and down?*
2. Find out what children know about spiders. *Where do they live? What do they eat? How do they move? How many legs do they have?* If photos of spiders are available, use them to stimulate discussion.
3. Sing the song, substituting "teeny weeny" for "itsy bitsy." Use a teeny weeny voice. Try substituting "big, gigantic" for "itsy bitsy" and sing in a big, gigantic voice.

Phonological Awareness

1. Discuss the rhyming words "itsy bitsy" and "teeny weeny." Invite the children to make up a rhyming word that goes with their name, for example, Evan bevan, Madison radison, Sam ham, or Quinn fin.

Learning Centers

Discovery (Out Came the Sun)

Place a shallow tray of water outdoors in the sun. *What happens to the water? How long does it take for the water to completely evaporate?*

Dramatic Play (Shadow Spiders)

Provide a light source. Encourage the children to wiggle their fingers like spiders and then to place their hands between the light source and the wall to create shadow spiders crawling up and down the wall.

Science (Down Came the Rain)

Give the children spray bottles of water and cookie sheets. Encourage them to spray the water on the cookie sheet using different intensity settings on the spouts. Ask them to describe the sounds that are made by each setting. *Which setting creates the loudest sound? Which setting creates the softest sound? Which setting sounds most like rain?* Call attention to the trails of water that are made as the water drops roll down the cookie sheet.

Writing (I Can Spell "Itsy Bitsy")

Provide magnetic letters and the words "Itsy Bitsy" written on chart paper or index cards. Encourage the children to use the magnetic letters to copy the words.

 **SEE ALSO**
"Mosquitoes" p. 113
"Shoo Fly" p. 112

Outdoor Play or Music and Movement Activity

1. Take the children on a nature walk to look for spiders or spider homes. Take a clipboard, paper, and pencil with you so you can make a list of the spider things you find.

2. Play "Itsy Bitsy Spider" on Thomas Moore's *Singing, Moving and Learning* CD. Encourage the children to dance like spiders. *Do you think having eight legs makes it more or less difficult to dance? Why?*

3. Have a water play day. Invite the children to wear their swimsuits and play in the sprinkler. Be sure to use sunscreen and discuss the importance of always wearing it when in the sun. Call attention to the conditions of being wet (cool, slippery). If the sun is out, call attention to how quickly the sidewalks and outdoor toys dry.

4. Invite the children to dance and sing along to "Itsy Bitsy Spider" (*Singing, Moving, and Learning* CD, Thomas Moore), "Itsy Bitsy Spider" (*For the Children: 10th Anniversary Edition* CD), or "Itsy Bitsy Spider" (*Is Everybody Happy?* CD, Jean Feldman).

REFLECTIONS

What lesson can we learn from "Itsy Bitsy Spider"? (You may have to help the children see that the spider didn't give up. She was persistent and kept trying to reach her goal.) What things do you do that require you to be persistent?

What do you think the Itsy Bitsy Spider did while she was waiting for the sun to dry up the rain?

Jack-o-Lantern

Jack-o-Lantern
(Tune: Clementine)

Jack-o-lantern, Jack-o-lantern,
You are such a funny sight.
As you sit there in my window
Looking out into the night.

You were once a yellow pumpkin
Growing on a sturdy vine.
Now you are my Jack-o-lantern.
Let your candlelight shine.

Related Songs, Chants, and Rhymes

Five Little Pumpkins

Five little pumpkins sitting on a gate. (hold up five fingers)
First one said, "Oh my, it's getting late." (wiggle first finger)
Second one said, "There are witches in the air." (wiggle second finger)
Third one said, "We don't care." (wiggle third finger)
Fourth one said, "Let's run, and run, and run." (wiggle fourth finger)
Fifth one said, "Oh, it's just Halloween fun." (wiggle fifth finger)
But whooo went the wind and out went the light (hold hands by sides of mouth
     and blow)
And five little pumpkins rolled out of sight. (roll hand over hand)

Five Waiting Pumpkins

(suit actions to words)

Five little pumpkins growing on a vine,
First one said, "It's time to shine!"
Second one said, "I love the fall"
Third one said, "I'm round as a ball."
Fourth one said, "I want to be a pie."
Fifth one said, "Let's say good-bye."

"Good-bye," said one!
"Adios," said two!
"Au revoir," said three!
"Ciao," said four!
"Aloha," said five!
And five little pumpkins were picked
that day!

THEME CONNECTIONS
Counting/Numbers
Growing Things
Holidays/Celebrations
Languages
Pumpkins
Sounds of Language

Literacy Activities

(Select one or two follow-up activities to do each time you sing a song or say a rhyme.)

Oral Language Development

1. Discuss words that may be new vocabulary for the children, such as "Jack-o-lantern," "sturdy," "vine," and "candlelight."

Phonological Awareness

1. Point out the rhyming words in the song (sight/night, vine/shine).

Learning Centers

Art (Finger Paint Faces)

Provide orange fingerpaint and let the children paint directly on the tabletop. Encourage them to make Jack-o-lanterns. Transfer their drawings to paper by pressing a sheet of clean paper on top of the fingerpaint drawing and then carefully lifting it up.

Discovery (Jack-o-Lantern)

Invite the children to help carve a real Jack-o-lantern. Discuss the steps you use to create the Jack-o-lantern. Ask questions while you work. *How is the texture of the outside of the pumpkin different from the inside of the pumpkin? How many seeds do you think are inside the pumpkin? How are oranges and pumpkins alike or different?*

Gross Motor (Toss a Match)

Draw several different Jack-o-lantern faces on a sheet of butcher paper. Draw matching faces on index cards. Have the children take turns picking up an index card. Encourage them to visually pick the matching face on the butcher paper, and then toss a beanbag on it.

Language (Build Your Own Face)

Cut out several pumpkins from orange felt and a variety of facial features from yellow and black felt. Encourage the children to create Jack-o-lantern faces. Ask the children to describe the faces they create.

Outdoor Play or Music and Movement Activity

1. Have a Pumpkin Relay Race. Divide the class into two groups. Place each group in a line and give each group a small pumpkin or a ball. Use yarn to create a start line and a turn-around line, about 10' apart. One child from each team rolls the pumpkin from the start line to the turn-around line and back to the start line. The first team to have all members complete the roll wins the game.
2. Sing along to "Five Little Pumpkins" (*Singable Songs for the Very Young* CD, Raffi).

REFLECTIONS

What kind of face do you like on your Jack-o-lantern? A funny face? A scary face? A mean face? A goofy face?

Could we make a Jack-o-lantern face on an apple? How?

K-K-K-Katy

K-K-K-Katy
(Tune: Traditional)

K-K-K-Katy, beautiful Katy,
You're the only g-g-g-girl that I adore;
When the m-m-m-moon shines over the cow shed.
I'll be waiting at the k-k-k-kitchen door.

Related Songs, Chants, and Rhymes

Bubble Song by Pam Schiller (Tune: K-K-K-Katy)

B-B-B-Bubbles, beautiful bubbles.
We love you more and more and more and more and more.
B-B-B—Bubbles, beautiful bubbles.
You're the b-b-b-bubbles we adore.

Little Boy Blue

Little Boy Blue, come blow your horn,
The sheep's in the meadow, the cow's in the corn.
Where's the little boy that looks after the sheep?
He's under the haystack, fast asleep!

THEME CONNECTIONS
Animals
Colors
Farms
Humor
Let's Pretend
Nursery Rhymes
Real and Make-
  Believe

SEE ALSO
"Lavender's Blue"
  p. 127
"Red River Valley"
  p. 98

Literacy Activities

(Select one or two follow-up activities to do each time you sing a song or say a rhyme.)

Oral Language Development

1. Discuss words that may be new vocabulary, such as "adore" and "cow shed."
2. Tell them that they are going to pretend that Katy is a cow instead of a woman. *Is that funny?* Ask the children to describe what Katy the cow might look like. *Does she have big eyes like most cows? Does she have long eyelashes?*

Comprehension

1. Explain that "K-K-K-Katy" is a love song and that a man in love with a woman named Katy wrote it. Many songs are about loving someone or something. Ask the children if they can think of another song about love (for example, "I Love the Mountains," "The Color Song," and "The Iguana in Lavender Socks").

Letter Knowledge and Recognition

1. Clap out the syllables to "Katy." Substitute some of the children's names that also have two syllables. For example, sing "J-J-J-Judy, beautiful Judy" or "M-M-M-Megan, beautiful Megan." For boys, change the words a bit. For example, try singing, "B-B-B-Bobby, good-looking, Bobby."

Learning Centers

Art (Katy Portraits)

Invite the children to draw a picture of what they think Katy the cow might look like. *Does she have big eyes? Is she brown? Is she black and white?*

Blocks (Barn Raising)

Invite the children to build a barn (cow shed) for Katy. Provide photographs of barns and cow sheds, if available. *What does Katy need? A place to sleep? Food?*

Games (Katy Puzzles)

Use the pattern of Katy (appendix p. 236) to make a puzzle. Make two or three copies, color them, laminate them, and cut them into puzzle pieces. If desired, glue large wiggle eyes on top of the drawn eyes. Invite the children to work the puzzles.

Writing (My Favorite Things)

Invite the children to name things that they adore. Make a list of the things as the children list them. Encourage them to illustrate their responses.

Outdoor Play or Music and Movement Activity

1. Blow bubbles. Sing "Bubble Song" (see Related Songs/Chants/Rhymes) while they chase the bubbles.

REFLECTIONS

If you were singing a song to someone you adore, to whom would you sing?

What letter does Katy's name start with?

Little Ducky Duddle

Little Ducky Duddle
(Tune: Traditional)

Little Ducky Duddle went wading in a puddle,
Went wading in a puddle quite small.
"Quack, quack!" said he,
"It doesn't really matter how much I splash and splatter.
I'm only a ducky after all. Quack, quack!"

Related Songs, Chants, and Rhymes

Six White Ducks (Tune: Traditional)

Six white ducks that I once knew,
Fat ducks, skinny ducks, they were, too.
But the one little duck with the feather on her back,
She ruled the others with a quack, quack, quack!
Quack, quack, quack,
Quack, quack, quack,
She ruled the others with a quack, quack, quack!

Down to the river they would go,
Wibble, wobble, wibble, wobble all in a row.
But the one little duck with the feather on her back,
She ruled the others with a quack, quack, quack!
Quack, quack, quack,
Quack, quack, quack,
She ruled the others with a quack, quack, quack!

THEME CONNECTIONS

Animal Sounds
Animals
Birds
Counting/Numbers
Rivers
Time of Day

SEE ALSO
"Be Kind to Your
   Web-Footed
   Friends" p. 60
"Five Little Ducks"
   p. 60

Home from the river they would come
Wibble, wobble, wibble, wobble, ho, hum, hum.
But the one little duck with the feather on her back,
She ruled the others with a quack, quack, quack!
Quack, quack, quack,
Quack, quack, quack,
She ruled the others with a quack, quack, quack!

Downy Duck

One day I saw a downy duck
With feathers on his back.
I said, "Good morning, downy duck."
And he said, "Quack, quack, quack."

Literacy Activities

(Select one or two follow-up activities to do each time you sing a song or say a rhyme.)

Oral Language Development

1. Discuss the words that may be new vocabulary for the children ("puddle" and "splatter").
2. Find out what children know about ducks. *Where do they live? What colors are they? What do they eat? How do they move?*

Phonological Awareness

1. Call attention to the words "splash" and "splatter." They are both examples of **onomatopoeia**—they sound like what they are describing. *What other sounds might someone make if they were playing in the water?*

Letter Knowledge and Recognition

1. Write the words "Ducky Duddle" on chart paper. Ask the children to identify the first letter in each word. Point out that this is an example of **alliteration**, consecutive words that begin with the same letter sound. Ask the children if they can think of other famous ducks that have first and last names that begin with the same letters (Donald Duck, Daisy Duck, Daffy Duck).
2. Write the tongue twister below on chart paper. Underline the first letter in each word. Point out that a tongue twister is a good example of alliteration.

    Ducky Duddle does dozens of dives.

Learning Centers

Art (Splatter Painting)

Invite the children to splatter paint. If you don't have a splatter paint screen, you can get the same effect with a strainer and a toothbrush. Dip a toothbrush in paint. Hold the strainer over a sheet of paper and rub the toothbrush on the strainer.

Gross Motor (Puddle Jump)

Cut out some puddles from blue butcher paper. Lay them on the floor several feet apart. Invite the children to jump over the puddles.

Water Play (Duck Puddles)

Show the children how to shape clay into a "puddle." Make a ball of clay, flatten it, and then punch in the center (similar to pushing in the center of mashed potatoes to add gravy). Fill the puddle with water. If small rubber ducks are available, they might fit in the puddle. Talk with the children as they make their puddles. *What would you do if you were allowed to play in a water puddle? What sounds do you think the water in the puddle might make? Have you ever jumped in a puddle?*

Writing (An Old Way to Write)

Show the children how a feather can be used as a quill. Write "Ducky Duddle" on a few index cards. Encourage them to use the quill to trace over "Ducky Duddle."

Outdoor Play or Music and Movement Activity

1. Play Duck, Duck, Goose. Children sit in a circle. One child, IT, walks around the outside of the circle, tapping each player on the head and saying "Duck." Eventually IT taps a player and says "Goose" instead. The tapped player gets up and chases IT around the circle. If she taps IT before they get around the circle, she gets to go back to her place. If she doesn't, she becomes the new IT and the game continues.
2. If weather permits, allow the children to make mud pies while playing outdoors.
3. Sing along with "Five Little Ducks" (*Where Is Thumbkin?* CD, Kimbo) or (*Songs Children Love to Sing* CD, Thomas Moore), or "Little White Duck" (*A Whole Lot of Animals* CD, Joel Reese).

REFLECTIONS

What would you do if you could play in a puddle? Would you splash the water? Have you ever played in a puddle?

What do you think it would be like to have wings instead of hands?

Little Skunk's Hole

Little Skunk's Hole
(Tune: Dixie)

Oh, I stuck my head
In the little skunk's hole,
And the little skunk said,
"Well, bless my soul!
Take it out! Take it out!
Take it out! Remove it!"

Oh, I didn't take it out,
And the little skunk said,
"If you don't take it out
You'll wish you had.
Take it out! Take it out!"
Pheew! I removed it!

Related Songs, Chants, and Rhymes

Little Ant's Hill by Pam Schiller (Tune: Dixie)

Oh, I stuck my foot
On a little ant's hill,
And the little ant said,
"You better be still,
Take it off! Take it off!
Take it off! Remove it!"

Oh, I didn't take it off,
And the little ant said,
"If you don't take it off
You'll wish you had.
Take it off! Take it off!"
Ouch! I removed it!

Little Bee's Hive by Pam Schiller (Tune: Dixie)

Oh, I stuck my hand
In a little bee's hive,
And the little bee said,
"Goodness, alive!
Take it out! Take it out!
Take it out! Remove it!"

Oh, I didn't take it out,
And the little bee said,
"If you don't take it out
You'll wish you had.
Take it out! Take it out!"
Buzzz! I removed it!

THEME CONNECTIONS

Animals
Humor
Insects
Things That Go
    Together

140

Skunk Tongue Twister

A skunk sat on a stump,
The skunk thunk the stump stunk,
And the stump thunk the skunk stunk.

Literacy Activities

(Select one or two follow-up activities to do each time you sing a song or say a rhyme.)

Oral Language Development

1. If photos of skunks are available, use them to encourage discussion. *What colors are skunks? Where do they live?* Explain that skunks typically live under brush, in burrows under the ground, inside hollows of fallen trees, and so forth.

2. Sing all three songs, "Little Skunk's Hole," "Little Ant's Hill," and "Little Bee's Hive." Discuss the skunk's hole, ant's hill, and bee's hive. Explain that each of these locations is the habitat (home) of the animal.

3. Discuss the expletive phrases in each song: "Well, bless my soul," "Hey! Get off my hill," and "Goodness alive!" Explain that these phrases are often used to express excitement, fear, and anger. A good example for children might be how they respond when someone snatches a toy from their hand. They might say, "Give it back!"

Learning Centers

Discovery (The Sound of Trouble)

Explain to the children that when a skunk sprays someone or somethng with its nasty-smelling scent, it makes a hissing sound ("sssshh"). Provide some items that might make a similar sound, such as a turkey baster, squeeze bottle, eyedropper, and a paper sack (filled with air). Challenge the children to listen to the sounds they make with each item and decide if the sound might replicate the sound of a skunk spraying an intruder.

Language (Solutions)

Encourage the children to brainstorm a list of suggestions of other things the skunk could do to get people to leave him alone. Write their ideas on chart paper.

SEE ALSO
"Anthill" p. 20
"The Ants Go
    Marching" p. 20
"Baby Bumblebee"
    p. 29
"Little Ants" p. 21

Math (Head in a Hole)

Cut a 12"-diameter hole in a piece of poster board or cardboard to represent a skunk's hole. Invite the children to see if their head will fit through the hole. *Does it fit?* Provide the children with 12" pieces of yarn. Ask them to use the yarn to measure other things in the center to see what else might fit through the hole. Help them make a list of the things they find.

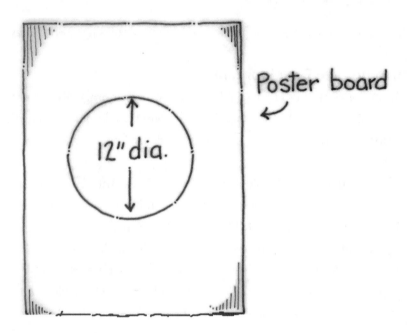

Writing (Puzzle Names)

Write the words "skunk," "ant," and "bee" on index cards. Make a second set of cards and cut each card into puzzle pieces (cut between the letters of the word). Challenge the children to put the puzzles together to spell the names of the animals.

Outdoor Play or Music and Movement Activity

1. Play Skunk Hole Miniature Golf. Place empty one-pound coffee cans on their sides to represent skunk holes. Provide children with tennis balls and a plastic bat or empty wrapping paper tube to use as a golf club. Number the holes 1-5 and have the children hit their ball into each hole (can). You can add obstacles in the pathways to increase difficulty.
2. Sing along with "Little Skunk's Hole" (*Here Is Thumbkin!* CD, Kimbo).

REFLECTIONS

Can you think of another animal that looks a little like a skunk? (cats, raccoons) In what ways do these animals look like a skunk?

Where do skunks live?

Miss Mary Mack

Miss Mary Mack

Miss Mary Mack, Mack, Mack
All dressed in black, black, black
With silver buttons, buttons, buttons
All down her back, back, back.
She asked her mother, mother, mother,
For fifty cents, cents, cents
To see the elephants, elephants, elephants
Jump the fence, fence, fence.
They jumped so high, high, high
They touched the sky, sky, sky
And they didn't come back, back, back
Till the fourth of July, ly, ly.

Related Songs, Chants, and Rhymes

Hey, Diddle Diddle

Hey diddle diddle,
The cat and the fiddle,
The cow jumped over the moon.
The little dog laughed to see such a sight,
And the dish ran away with the spoon.

Mary Had a Little Lamb (Tune: Traditional)

Mary had a little lamb, little lamb, little lamb.
Mary had a little lamb,
Its fleece was white as snow.

Everywhere that Mary went, Mary went, Mary went,
Everywhere that Mary went
The lamb was sure to go.

THEME CONNECTIONS
Animals
Colors
Holidays/Celebrations
Humor
Money
Nursery Rhymes
Real and Make-
    Believe
School
Sun, Moon, Stars

SEE ALSO

"Annie Mae" p. 17

"Lazy Mary" p. 26

"Michael Finnegan"
p. 35

Literacy Activities

(Select one or two follow-up activities to do each time you sing a song or say a rhyme.)

Phonological Awareness

1. Call attention to the rhyming words in the song: Mack/black/back, elephants/fence, and high/sky/July.

Letter Knowledge and Recognition

1. Write "Miss Mary Mack" on chart paper. Ask the children to identify the first letter in the first and last name. Explain that "Mary Mack" is an example of **alliteration**, consecutive words that begin with the same sound. Ask the children if they can name any favorite characters whose first and last names start with the same letter (Mickey Mouse, Donald Duck, Baby Bop, Big Bird). Challenge the children to think of an alliterative name for Barney or another favorite character.

Comprehension

1. Ask the children questions about the elephant jumping over the fence. *Would it be difficult for an elephant to jump over a fence? Why? Can an elephant jump over a fence?*

2. Ask about the factual and make-believe parts of the song. *Which things mentioned in the song could actually happen? Which things mentioned in the song are only make-believe?*

Learning Centers

Dramatic Play (All Dressed in Black)

Provide an assortment of black clothing and accessories for the children to explore. Encourage them to admire themselves in a mirror.

Fine Motor (Silver Buttons)

Give the children a collection of silver buttons to explore. Encourage them to sort the buttons by any criteria they choose, such as size, number of holes, ones they like, and so forth. Or give each child a small matchbox covered with contact paper and a silver button to go inside the box. Challenge them to show you the many different places they can put the button in relationship to the box (inside, outside, on top of, under, beside, over, and so on).

Gross Motor (Jumping the Fence)

Use blocks to construct a fence. Invite the children to take turns jumping over the "fence." *How would you jump over the fence if you were an elephant? What is different about an elephant jumping the fence? Do you think an elephant really could jump over a fence?*

Writing (Miss Mary Mack)

Write "Miss Mary Mack" on chart paper and encourage the children to copy it using magnetic letters.

Make a Gel Bag. Spoon ½ cup of hair gel into a zipper-closure plastic bag. Add a couple of tablespoons of black tempera paint. Seal shut with glue. Invite the children to make the letter "M" on the bags with their fingers.

Outdoor Play or Music and Movement Activity

1. Encourage the children to jump rope while chanting "Miss Mary Mack." Have two children swing the rope back and forth in a slow rhythmic pace while the other children jump it one at a time. Explain that the original "Miss Mary Mack" was a jump rope rhyme.
2. Encourage the children to create a "hand jive" to "Miss Mary Mack."
3. Sing along to "Miss Mary Mack" (*You Sing a Song, I'll Sing a Song* CD, Ella Jenkins), "Hey Diddle Diddle" (*Three Little Kittens* CD, Kimbo), or "Mary Had a Little Lamb" (*For Our Children: 10th Anniversary Edition* CD, Rhino).

REFLECTIONS

Who jumps over the fence in the song? Can you think of another song or rhyme where a big animal jumps over something? (Hey, Diddle Diddle)

Why did Miss Mary Mack ask for fifty cents? What would you do with fifty cents?

Mister Moon

Mister Moon
(Tune: Traditional)

Oh, Mister Moon, Moon,
Bright and shiny Moon
Won't you please
Shine down on me?

Oh, Mister Moon, Moon,
Bright and shiny Moon,
Won't you please
Set me fancy free?

I'd like to linger
But I've got to run,
Mama's callin'
"Baby get your homework done!"

Oh Mister Moon, Moon,
Bright and shiny Moon,
Won't you please

Shine down on me?
Talk about your shine on,
Please shine down on me.

Related Songs, Chants, and Rhymes

Mister Sun (Tune: Mister Moon)

Oh, Mister Sun, Sun, Mister Golden Sun
Won't you please shine down on me?
Oh, Mister Sun, Sun, Mister Golden Sun
Hiding behind that tree.

These little children are asking you
To please come out so we can play with you.
Oh, Mister Sun, Sun, Mister Golden Sun,
Won't you please shine down on me?

Literacy Activities

(Select one or two follow-up activities to do each time you sing a song or say a rhyme.)

Comprehension

1. Ask the children about the bright and shiny moon mentioned in the song.
   What does it look like? Can you see it in the daylight?

THEME CONNECTIONS

Caring for Our
    World/Ecology
Day and Night
Opposites
Sun, Moon, Stars

Phonological Awareness

1. Write the words "Mister Moon" on chart paper. Ask the children to identify the letters in each word that are the same. Underline the beginning letters. Remind the children that when consecutive words begin with the same letter sound, it is called **alliteration**. Ask them if they can think of other words to go with moon that would be alliterative (for example, mighty moon, magnificent moon, magic moon, and merry moon).

Print Awareness

1. Discuss daytime and nighttime activities. Encourage the children to brainstorm a list of activities appropriate for each.

Learning Centers

Construction (Night Skies)

Provide a flannel board, white felt cutouts of moons and stars, and a few gray felt cutouts of clouds. Encourage the children to create a night sky. Ask questions about the nighttime sky. *Where are the birds? Do airplanes fly at night? What happens to a night sky during a thunderstorm?*

Dramatic Play (Moon Shadows)

Provide a light source such as a large flashlight or an overhead projector. Encourage the children to make shadows on the wall by placing themselves between the light source and the wall. Ask them to describe the shadows they are making.

Language (Day and Night Stories)

Encourage the children to tell you which things they like to do during the day and which things they like to do at night. Make a personal list for each child.

Writing (I Can Spell "Moon" and "Sun")

Write the words "moon" and "sun" on chart paper or index cards. Provide blue fingerpaint directly on the tabletop. Encourage the children to write the words "moon" and "sun" in the paint using their index finger as a writing tool. Some children will be able to write the words. Suggest that they write the words on index cards and add them to their Word Box (shoebox collection of words they can write).

Outdoor Play or Music and Movement Activity

1. Play shadow tag. The children try to step on each other's shadows while running outdoors.
2. Sing along with "Mister Moon" (*Where Is Thumbkin?* CD) or "Mr. Sun" (*Singable Songs for the Very Young* CD, Raffi).

SEE ALSO

"Little Drop of
    Dew" p. 211

"Star Light, Star
    Bright" p. 211

"Twinkle, Twinkle
    Little Star"
    p. 211

BRAIN CONNECTION

Solar and lunar cycles play a major role in our biorhythms. These cycles contribute to our more alert and less alert periods of the day, as well as control our body's hormonal and chemical flows.

REFLECTIONS

Which activity is your favorite daytime activity? Why? Which activity is your favorite nighttime activity? Why?

How are day and night alike? How are they different?

The More We Get Together

The More We Get Together
(Tune: Traditional)

The more we get together,
Together, together.
The more we get together,
The happier we'll be.

For your friends are my friends,
And my friends are your friends.
The more we get together,
The happier we'll be.

Related Songs, Chants, and Rhymes

Five Friends Dancing in a Line by Pam Schiller

Five friends dancing in a line. (hold up five fingers)
They look great! They look fine! (hands out to side)
One is turning around and around. (hold up one finger and turn around)
One is jumping off the ground. (hold up two fingers and jump)
One is spinning across the floor. (hold up three fingers and spin)
One is twisting out the door. (hold up four fingers and twist)
And one is saying, "Let's dance some more!" (hold up five fingers and dance them on
    the floor)

For He's a Jolly Good Fellow (Tune: Traditional)

For he's a jolly good fellow,   *Which nobody can deny,*
For he's a jolly good fellow,   *Which nobody can deny,*
For he's a jolly good fellow,   *For he's a jolly good fellow,*
Which nobody can deny.   *Which nobody can deny.*

THEME CONNECTIONS
Emotions
Friends
Self-Esteem
Sun, Moon, Stars
Time of Day

Good Morning to You! (Tune: Traditional)

Good morning to you!
Good morning to you!
We're all in our places
With bright shining faces.
Oh, this is the way to start a great day!

Good noontime to you!
Good noontime to you!
We're all in our places
With food on our faces.
Oh, this is the way to have a great day!

Good evening to you!
Good evening to you!
Stars and moon in their places
They go through their paces.
Oh, this is the way to end a great day!

Make New Friends (Tune: Traditional)

Make new friends but keep the old.
One is silver and the other gold.

Side by Side (Tune: Traditional)

Oh, we ain't got a barrel of money
Maybe we're ragged and funny,
But we'll travel along, singing a song—side by side.

Chorus:
Through all kinds of weather,
What if the sky should fall
Just as long as we're together,
It doesn't matter at all.

No, we don't know what's coming tomorrow
Maybe it's trouble and sorrow,
But we'll travel the road, sharing our load—side by side.

Chorus

When they've all had their quarrels and parted
We'll be the same as we started
Just traveling along, singing a song—side by side.

SEE ALSO

"Hello, Good
Friends" p. 221

This Is Austin (Tune: The Mulberry Bush)

(Substitute names and characteristics for the children in your classroom.)

This is <u>Austin</u> over here.

He has on a <u>bright blue shirt</u>.

This is <u>Austin</u>, our new friend.

We're so glad he's here.

Literacy Activities

(Select one or two follow-up activities to do each time you sing a song or say a rhyme.)

Oral Language Development

1. Discuss friendship with the children. *What does it mean to be a friend? What responsibility do we have to our friends?*

2. Teach the children how to use American Sign Language (appendix p. 240) to say, "Hello, friend."

Comprehension

1. Ask the children questions about the song. *Why would getting together make us happy? Who do you enjoy getting together with? What do you and your friends do when you get together?*

Learning Centers

Art (My Friends and Me)

Encourage the children to draw a picture of something they enjoy doing with a friend. With permission, label the pictures as directed by each child.

Fine Motor (Name Puzzles)

Cut pieces of tagboard into 4" x 18" strips. Print each child's name on a strip, leaving enough space between the letters to draw puzzle lines. Laminate and cut into puzzle pieces. Provide a zipper-closure plastic bag for each child to use to store his or her name. Encourage the children to work their name puzzle and the name puzzle of a friend.

Games (Tic-Tac-Toe)

Show the children how to play Tic-Tac-Toe. Encourage them to play the game with a friend.

Math (Find a Friend)

Take photographs of the children (three to a photo). Cut out the faces of each child to make head shots. Tape the head shots to a sheet of paper and make multiple copies. Cut out the photos so that you have multiple copies of each child. Glue one photo of each child to a manila folder and laminate the rest of the photos of each child. Give the folder and the additional loose photos to the children and ask them to match the photos one to one. Ask questions. *How many friends do you have in the classroom? Who are your best friends?*

Outdoor Play or Music and Movement Activity

1. Invite the children to do a Friendship March. Ask them to select a friend, hold their friend's hand, and march together to some marching music.
2. Play Tummy Ticklers. Have all the children lay on the floor with their head on another child's tummy. When all the children are in position, say something funny. What happens?

3. Sing along with "Good Morning" (*Songs for the Whole Day* CD, Thomas Moore), "Make New Friends" (*Thinkable, Movable, Lovable Songs* CD, ProVideo Productions), or "The More We Get Together" (*Singable Songs for the Very Young* CD, Raffi).

Special Activity

Have a Friendship Tea. Ask the children to pick a friend to share punch and cookies with. Decorative plates and napkins will add fun to the party.

REFLECTIONS
What does it mean when you say someone is your friend? How do you treat your friends?

Can mommies and daddies be our friends? Why? Can our pets be our friends?

My Hand on Myself

My Hand on Myself
(Tune: Traditional)

My hand on my head, (place one hand on head)
What have I here? (open arms palm up)
This is my head thinker (or topnotcher) (point to head)
Mama, my dear.
Head thinker, head thinker (or topnotcher), (point to head again)
Dickie, dickie, doo (knock on head)
That's what I learned in school. (shake index finger)
Boom! Boom!

My hand on my brow, (place hand on brow)
What have I here? (open arms palm up)
This is my sweat boxer, (point to forehead)
Mama, my dear.
Sweat boxer, head thinker (or topnotcher),
     (point to head and then forehead)
Dickie, dickie, doo (knock on head)
That's what I learned in school. (shake index finger)
Boom! Boom!

(continue adding body parts and suit hand
motions to words)
Eye—eye blinker
Nose—nose blower
Mouth—milk pusher or food grinder
Chin—chin chopper
Heart—chest ticker
Stomach—bread basket
Knees—knee benders
Toes—pedal pushers

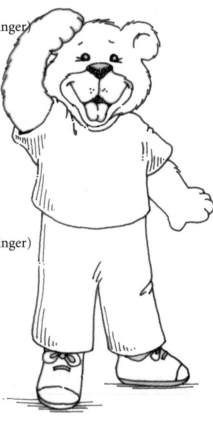

THEME CONNECTIONS
Humor
Parts of the Body
School
Self

152

Related Songs, Chants, and Rhymes

I Can, You Can! by Pam Schiller

I can put my hands up high. Can you?

I can wink my eye. Can you?

I can stick out my tongue. Can you?

I can nod my head. Can you?

I can kiss my toe. Can you?

I can pull on my ear. Can you?

I can wrinkle my nose. Can you?

I can give myself a great big hug. Can you?

And if I give my hug to you, will you give yours to me?

I Like School by Pam Schiller

I like school,

I like it a lot.

It's my favorite place,

Believe it or not.

I love blowing bubbles.

I love all the toys.

I love the quiet,

And I love the noise.

I love painting with feathers

And building with blocks.

Reading good books

And dancing in socks.

My teacher loves me.

I know that it's true.

She smiles and laughs

The whole day through.

I'm a (insert the name of your school)

student,

It's plain to see,

Cause I'm just as happy

As a kid can be.

My Body Talks by Pam Schiller

(suit the actions to the words)

When I want to say "hello," I wave my hand like this.

When I want to say "no," I shake my head from side to side.

When I want to say "yes," I nod my head up and down.

When I want to say "I'm mad," I stomp my foot.

When I am really happy, my face lights up with a grin.

When I want to say "good job," I stick up my thumb.

When I want to celebrate a success, I clap my hands.

When I want to say "come here," I wave my hand toward me.

When I want to say "I love you," I put my arms around you and squeeze.

When I want to say "good-bye," I wave my hand and blow you a kiss.

My Hand on Myself (Bilingual version) (Tune: My Hand on My Head)

(suit the actions to the words)
My hands on my head,
¿Que esta aqui?
This is my cabeza,
My mamacita.
Cabeza, cabeza, la, la, la, la,
That's what I learned in my school.
¡Sí! ¡Sí!

My hands on my eyes,
¿Que esta aqui?
These are my ojos,
My mamacita.
Cabeza, ojos, la, la, la, la,
That's what I learned in my school.
¡Sí! ¡Sí!

My hands on my ears,
¿Que esta aqui?
These are my orejas,
My mamacita.
Cabeza, ojos, orejas, la, la, la, la,
That's what I learned in my school.
¡Sí! ¡Sí!

Nose—nariz
Mouth—boca
Stomach—stomago
Feet—pies

Literacy Activities

(Select one or two follow-up activities to do each time you sing a song or say a rhyme.)

Oral Language Development

1. Discuss the terms used for body parts in the song. Explain that the names for the various body parts are a reflection of how that part of the body is used. For example, "head thinker" is used because we use our head (brain) to think. "Nose blower" is used because we can blow our nose.

2. Encourage the children to talk about the kind of things that they learn at school.

Phonological Awareness

1. Write "Dickie, dickie, doo" on a piece of chart paper. Ask the children to identify the first letter in each word. *What sound do you hear at the beginning of each word?* Tell the children that these words are an example of **alliteration.** The repetition of the same sound at the beginning of several word is called **alliteration.**

2. Encourage the children to clap the syllables they hear in each of the words used to describe the different body parts, such as "head thinker," "sweat boxer," "eye blinker," "nose blower," and so on.

Learning Centers

Gross Motor (Knee Benders)

Make a tunnel out of boxes or by putting a sheet over a table. Encourage the children to crawl through the tunnel. Ask them which body parts they use when they crawl. *Can you crawl without bending your knees?*

Science (Chest Ticker)

Provide a stethoscope for the children to use to listen to their heartbeats ("chest ticker"). Talk with them about what they hear. *Is your heartbeat fast or slow? Is it loud or soft?*

Snack (Milk Pusher)

Provide milk and two flavorings (chocolate and strawberry). Let the children make flavored milk or keep it as is. Help the children create a graph that shows which type of milk they drank (including unflavored).

Writing (New Body Language)

Write each one of the body part names used in the song on a piece of chart paper. Invite the children to copy any of the words they are interested in copying using crayons or magnetic letters.

Outdoor Play or Music and Movement Activity

1. Play Simon Says using the song terms for body parts. Choose one child to be "Simon." All the other children stand side-by-side in a line facing Simon. "Simon" gives the other children orders that they must carry out, but only when the orders follow the phrase "Simon says..." (e.g., "Simon says touch your nose blower"). If a child follows an order that Simon did not say (e.g., "Pat your bread basket"), then he is out and must sit down. The last child standing becomes the new Simon for the next game of "Simon Says."

2. Discuss the song's term for feet ("pedal pushers") while the children are riding tricycles. *Is "pedal pusher" a good name for feet?*

BRAIN CONNECTION

When teaching the children about their bodies and how to care for them, be sure to include the brain. Help children understand that both water and oxygen help them think better. Explain that food keeps their brain working to its best capability and that rest is needed so the brain has time to organize the things that we learn.

REFLECTIONS

Do you like the terms used in the song for body parts? Why? Why not? Which term do you like best? Why?

What new information did you learn about your body today?

Old MacDonald Had a Farm

Old MacDonald Had a Farm

(Tune: Traditional)

Old MacDonald had a farm, E-I-E-I-O
And on this farm she had a cow, E-I-E-I-O
With a moo, moo here,
And a moo, moo there,
Here a moo, there a moo,
Everywhere a moo, moo.
Old MacDonald had a farm, E-I-E-I-O!

Additional verses:
Pig—oink, oink
Cat—meow, meow
Dog—bow-wow
Horse—neigh, neigh

Related Songs, Chants, and Rhymes

Farm Colors (Tune: Bingo)

There was a farmer had a bird,
And Blue was his name-o.
B-L-U-E!
B-L-U-E!
B-L-U-E!
And Blue was his name-o.

There was a farmer had a pig,
And Red was her name-o.
R-E-D!
R-E-D!
R-E-D!
And Red was her name-o.

There was a farmer had a chick,
And Yellow was his name-o.
Y-E-L-L-O-W!
Y-E-L-L-O-W!
Y-E-L-L-O-W!
And Red was his name-o.

There was a farmer had a horse,
And Green was her name-o.
G-R-E-E-N!
G-R-E-E-N!
G-R-E-E-N!
And Green was her name-o.

THEME CONNECTIONS
Animals
Families
Farms

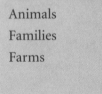

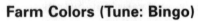
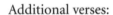

There was a farmer had a duck,
And Orange was his name-o.
O-R-A-N-G-E!
O-R-A-N-G-E!
O-R-A-N-G-E!
And Orange was her name-o.

There was a farmer had a cow,
And Purple was his name-o.
P-U-R-P-L-E!
P-U-R-P-L-E!
P-U-R-P-L-E!
And Purple was his name-o.

There was a farmer had a cat,
And Black was her name-o!
B-L-A-C-K
B-L-A-C-K
B-L-A-C-K
And Black was her name-o.

Farmer in the Dell (Tune: Traditional)

The farmer in the dell,
The farmer in the dell,
Heigh-ho the derry-o,
The farmer in the dell.

Additional verses:
The farmer takes a wife...
The wife takes a child...
The child takes a nurse...
The nurse takes a cat...
The cat takes a mouse...
The mouse takes the cheese...
The cheese stands alone...

(Change the words of the song to reflect gender differences. For example, if the farmer is a female, she will take a husband, not wife.)

Ten children (or more) join hands and dance around the farmer, who stands in the center of the circle as they sing. At the end of the first verse, the farmer chooses his wife, who joins him in the circle. At the end of the next verse, the wife chooses a child, and so on, until the last verse when everyone is in the circle except the cheese, who stands alone in the middle of the circle. Whoever winds up being the cheese becomes the farmer for the next round.

Old MacDonald Has a Band (Tune: Old MacDonald Had a Farm)

Old MacDonald has a band, mi, mi, re, re, do.

And in his band he has some drums, mi, mi, re, re, do.

With a rum-tum here,

And a rum-tum there,

Here a rum, there a tum,

Everywhere a rum-tum.

Old MacDonald has a band,

The best band in the land.

Other verses:

…he has some flutes…with a toot-toot…

…he has some fiddles…with a zing-zing…

Literacy Activities

(Select one or two follow-up activities to do each time you sing a song or say a rhyme.)

Oral Language Development

1. Find out what the children know about farms. *What animals live on the farm? What happens on the farm? What does the farmer do?*

Letter Knowledge and Recognition

1. Change the "E-I-E-I-O" in the song to another letter variation, such as "A-I-A-I-O," "B-I-B-I-O," "C-I-C-I-O," and "D-I-D-I-O."

Learning Centers

Art (Cow-Assisted Art)

Provide a small saucer of buttermilk and chalk and invite the children to experiment with buttermilk art. Show them how to dip their chalk in the buttermilk and then draw on their paper. Talk with them about where buttermilk comes from.

Dramatic Play (Old MacDonald Dress-Up)

Provide farming clothes for the children to use for dress-up play. You might consider a straw hat, overalls, boots, bandana, work gloves, and an old shirt. Talk with the children while they play. Explain the purpose the clothing item serves for the farmer.

Games (Chicken Feather Race)

Place two chicken feathers on a table and invite two children to participate in a feather race. Each child blows his or her feather and attempts to be the first one to blow his or her feather off the table.

Writing (E-I-E-I-O)

Write "E-I-E-I-O" on an index card. Provide magnetic letters and encourage the children to copy the letters. Encourage them to experiment with other letter combinations.

Outdoor Play or Music and Movement Activity

1. Invite the children to play "Farmer in the Dell." Choose one child to be the Farmer. The other children walk in a circle around the Farmer as they sing the song together. See Related Songs, Chants, and Rhymes above for the words to the song and the description of movements.

2. Try some of these music and movement ideas:
   - Play "Old MacDonald Had a Farm" or "Farmer in the Dell" (*Songs Children Love to Sing* CD, Thomas Moore). Invite the children to sing along with these instrumental versions of the song.
   - Sing along with "Mr. Bristol Goes to the Zoo" (*I Am Special* CD, Thomas Moore), "The Farmer in the Dell" (*Esté es mí tierra* CD, José Lluis Orozco), or "Old MacDonald's Band" (*Singable Songs for the Very Young* CD, Raffi).

REFLECTIONS

Why doesn't Old MacDonald have any giraffes and elephants on his farm?

Which farm animal is your favorite?

Open, Shut Them

Open, Shut Them
(Tune: Traditional)

(suit hand motions to words)
Open, shut them.
Open, shut them.
Give a little clap. (clap)
Open, shut them.
Open, shut them.
Put them in your lap.

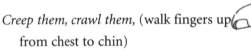

Creep them, crawl them, (walk fingers up
    from chest to chin)
Creep them, crawl them.
Right up to your chin
Open up your little mouth, (open your mouth)
But do not let them in.

Falling, falling,
Falling, falling
Right down to the ground. (touch the ground with fingers)
Then you pick them up again,
    (bring hands back to lap)
And turn them round and round.

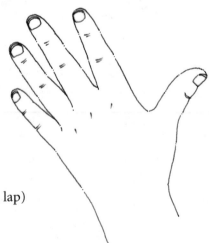

Faster, faster,
Faster, faster
Give a little clap. (clap faster)
Slower, slower,
Slower, slower
Place them in your lap. (place hands in lap)

THEME CONNECTIONS

Counting/Numbers
Opposites
Parts of the Body
Self-Esteem
Senses
Sounds and
    Movement

Related Songs, Chants, and Rhymes

Clap Your Hands

(suit movements to words)

Clap your hands 1-2-3.

Clap your hands just like me.

Wiggle your fingers 1-2-3.

Wiggle your fingers just like me.

Soft Touches by Pam Schiller

I love soft things

Very much.

Soft things to feel,

Soft things to touch.

My kitten's fur,

A gentle breeze,

A bedtime kiss,

I love all these.

A feather pillow,

A furry muff,

A baby's cheek,

A powder puff.

SEE ALSO

"Head, Shoulders, Baby" p. 91

"Head, Shoulders, Knees, and Toes" p. 91

"I Can, You Can!" p. 153

"My Body Talks" p. 153

"Where Is Thumbkin?" p. 220

These Little Hands of Mine by Pam Schiller

These little hands of mine

Can do things, oh, so fine.

They can reach way out,

They can reach way up.

They can hold a crayon,

They can hold a cup.

They can open and close.

They can grab your nose.

These little hands of mine

Can do things, oh, so fine.

They can tell what's cold,

They can tell what's hot.

They can tell what's sticky,

They can tell what's not.

They can say, "What's that?"

They can pet the cat.

They can give a big "Hi!"

They can wave good-bye.

Literacy Activities

(Select one or two follow-up activities to do each time you sing a song or say a rhyme.)

Oral Language Development

1. Discuss "open" and "shut." Ask the children to come up with several examples of things that open and shut.
2. Discuss the words "creep" and "crawl." Ask volunteers to demonstrate creeping and crawling. *How are they different from one another?* Invite the children to add a new verse specifying another way the finger could get from their lap to their chin (e.g., walk, skip, hop, twist, and so forth).

Letter Knowledge and Recognition

1. Write the word "open" on chart paper or on the chalkboard. Ask the children to identify the letters in the word. Ask them where they might see "Open" signs. *What do the signs mean?*

Learning Centers

Art (Creep and Crawl Art)

Provide fingerpaint. Encourage the children to make a picture by creeping their fingers back and forth across the paper. Ask them to make a second print by crawling their fingers (let the children decide how to do this) across the paper. *Do the pictures look different? How?*

Blocks (Challenging Towers)

Challenge the children to build a tower with their eyes shut. Have them build a second tower with their eyes open. Ask questions. *Which tower was easier to build? How did you know where to put the blocks when you had your eyes shut?*

Games (Which Hand?)

Teach the children how to play Which Hand? Place your hands behind your back and hide a button in one hand. Then hold your hands (in fists) out in front of you and let one of the children guess which hand is holding the button. Let the children continue playing the game with partners.

Gross Motor (Creeping and Crawling)

Use masking tape to make a 12' line on the floor. Invite the children to crawl down the line and then to creep down the line. *Which way of traveling the line is easier? Which is faster?*

Outdoor Play or Music and Movement Activity

1. Invite the children to creep (stand on tiptoes and walk) across the playground and then run back across. *Which takes more time: creeping or running?*
2. Try some of these music and movement ideas:
   - Invite the children to do "The Finger Dance" (*My Magical World* CD, Thomas Moore.)
   - Sing along with "Open, Shut Them" (*Where Is Thumbkin?* CD, Kimbo) or
   - Open, Shut Them" (*Thinkable, Movable, Lovable Songs* CD, ProVideo Productions).

BRAIN CONNECTION

The finger muscles are associated with memory. Using our fingers during learning activities helps boost our ability to remember what we are learning.

REFLECTIONS

What did you learn today about creeping and crawling?

What body parts can you open and shut? (mouth, eyes, hands, legs)

Over the River and Through the Woods

Over the River and Through the Woods
(Tune: Traditional)

Over the river and through the woods,
To grandmother's (or grandfather's) house we go;
The horse knows the way
To carry the sleigh,
Through the white and drifted snow, oh!

Over the river and through the woods,
Oh, how the wind does blow!
It stings the toes,
And bites the nose,
As over the ground we go.

Over the river and through the woods,
To have a first-rate play;
Oh, hear the bell ring,
"Ting-a-ling-ling!"
Hurrah for Thanksgiving Day-ay!

Over the river and through the woods,
Trot fast my dapple gray!
Spring over the ground,
Like a hunting hound!
For this is Thanksgiving Day.

THEME CONNECTIONS
Animals
Clothing
Families
Food
Holidays/Celebrations
Humor
Parts of the Body
Seasons
Weather

Related Songs, Chants, and Rhymes

Grandpa's (or Grandma's) Glasses

These are Grandpa's glasses. (make glasses with fingers)
This is Grandpa's hat. (tap head)
This is how he folds his hands, (fold hands and place in lap)
And puts them in his lap.

SEE ALSO
"Five Fat Turkeys
     Are We" p. 58
"Mighty Fine
     Turkey" p. 58

She'll Be Comin' 'Round the Mountain (Tune: Traditional)

She'll be comin' 'round the mountain when she comes.
She'll be comin' 'round the mountain when she comes.—"Toot, toot" (pull an
     imaginary whistle)
She'll be comin' 'round the mountain,
She'll be comin' 'round the mountain,
She'll be comin' 'round the mountain when she comes.—"Toot, toot" (pull an
     imaginary whistle)

She'll be driving six white horses when she comes.—"Whoa back!" (pull back reins)
She'll be driving six white horses when she comes.
She'll be driving six white horses,
She'll be driving six white horses,
She'll be driving six white horses when she comes.—"Whoa back!" (pull back reins)

Additional verses:
And we'll all go out to meet her when she comes.—"Hi, babe!" (wave hello)…
We will all have chicken and dumplin's when she comes.—"Yum, yum" (rub
     tummy)…
She'll be wearing red pajamas when she comes.—"Scratch, scratch." (scratch)…
She'll have to sleep with Grandma when she comes.—"Move over" (make pushing
     motions)…
We'll have a great big party when she comes.—"Yahoo!" (swing arm over head for a
     lasso)…

This Is the Way We Pack for Travel by Pam Schiller
(Tune: Here We Go 'Round the Mulberry Bush)

This is the way we pack for travel,
Pack for travel, pack for travel.
This is the way we pack for travel
When it's time to go away.

Additional verses:
We put our clothes in nice and neat…
We get our toothbrush and some soap…
We pack our brush and our comb…
We sneak our favorite toys inside…

Through the Woods by Pam Schiller
(Tune: Over the River and Through the Woods)

Over the river and through the woods,
To grandmother's house I go.
The path leads the way to follow and play
Through the dark and scary woods, yes!

Over the river and through the woods,
I'm frightened I confess.
But I will not stop and I will not talk,
As along the path I walk.
* Adapted to accompany "Little Red Riding Hood"

Literacy Activities

(Select one or two follow-up activities to do each time you sing a song or say a rhyme.)

Oral Language Development

1. Discuss words in the song that may be new vocabulary for the children, for example, "drifted snow," "sleigh," "dapple gray," and "hunting hound."
2. Talk about the many ways children may travel to see their grandparents.

Print Awareness

1. Encourage the children to brainstorm a list of the reasons they may go visit their grandparents (e.g., holidays, vacation, to bring them something, and so on). Call attention to some of the letters as you are writing. If you use numbers, point them out. Read the list to the children when you are finished.

Letter Knowledge and Recognition

1. Write "grandmother" and "grandfather" on chart paper. Compare the words. *Which letters are the same? What is the first letter of each name?* Make a list of names that children call their grandparents.

Learning Centers

Art (A Snowy Day)

Make Puff Paint by mixing ½ cup of glue, 2 tablespoons of white tempera paint, and 2 cups of shaving cream. Provide white Puff Paint and blue construction paper and encourage the children to fingerpaint snowy day pictures. Ask questions about snow as they work. *Can you show me what "drifted snow" looks like? Have you ever seen snow? Where? Did you touch it? What did it feel like? Did you play in the snow?*

Dramatic Play (Packing for a Visit)

Provide suitcases, clothing, and accessories. Encourage the children to pretend they are going for a visit and need to pack their suitcases. Talk with the children about what kinds of things are important to include.

Gross Motor (Sleigh Rides)

Attach heavy yarn or rope to one end of several shallow boxes to make sleighs. Invite the children to pull stuffed animals in the sleighs.

Writing (Special Names)

Place the list of names that children call their grandmother and grandfather (See previous page, Letter Knowledge and Recognition). Encourage the children to find the name or names they use and copy them using magnetic letters or alphabet letter patterns (appendix p. 232).

Outdoor Play or Music and Movement Activity

1. Play a teacher-directed game of Grandmother, May I? The teacher is grandmother. The children stand in a line side-by-side facing you. Call out to them one at a time, asking them to make some type of movement (such as hop, take baby steps, walk backwards, touch their nose, and so forth). Children follow the direction only after asking, "Grandmother, may I?" If they move without first asking permission, they are out of the game.

2. Invite the children to sing along with "Comin' 'Round the Mountain" (*Songs Children Love to Sing* CD), "Over the River and Through the Woods" (*Three Little Kittens* CD, Kimbo), "Comin' 'Round the Mountain" (*Rockin' Rhymes and Good Ol' Times* CD, Jean Feldman), "She'll Be Coming Around the Mountain" (*Walt Disney Records: Children's Favorite Songs, Vol. 1* CD), or "Over the River and Through the Woods" (*Walt Disney Records: Children's Favorite Songs, Vol. 3* CD).

REFLECTIONS

How is a sleigh ride different from a car ride?

What is the best thing about a trip to grandmother and/or grandfather's house?

Peanut Butter

Peanut Butter

Chorus:
Peanut, peanut butter—jelly!
Peanut, peanut butter—jelly!

First you take the peanuts and
You dig 'em, you dig 'em.
(pretend to dig peanuts)
Dig 'em, dig 'em, dig 'em.
Then you smash 'em, you smash 'em.
(pretend to smash peanuts)
Smash 'em, smash 'em, smash 'em.
Then you spread 'em, you spread 'em.
(pretend to spread the peanuts)
Spread 'em, spread 'em, spread 'em.

Chorus

Then you take the berries and (pretend to pick berries)
You pick 'em, you pick 'em.
Pick 'em, pick 'em, pick 'em.
Then you smash 'em, you smash 'em. (pretend to smash berries)
Smash 'em, smash 'em, smash 'em.
Then you spread 'em, you spread 'em. (pretend to spread berries)
Spread 'em, spread 'em, spread 'em.

Chorus

Then you take the sandwich and
You bite it, you bite it. (pretend to bite a sandwich)
Bite it, bite it, bite it.
Then you chew it, you chew it. (pretend to chew a sandwich)
Chew it, chew it, chew it.
Then you swallow it, you swallow it. (pretend to swallow peanut butter sandwich)
Swallow it, swallow it, swallow it.

Hum chorus

THEME CONNECTIONS
Cooking
Food
Humor
Things I Like/
    Favorite Things
Trains
Travel/Transportation

Related Songs, Chants, and Rhymes

Found a Peanut (Tune: Clementine)

SEE ALSO

"Chocolate Rhyme"
p. 39

"The Ice Cream
Chant" p. 39

"Peas Porridge,
Hot" p. 39

"Rima de
Chocolate"
p. 40

Found a peanut, found a peanut,
Found a peanut just now,
Oh, I just now found a peanut,
Found a peanut just now.

Cracked it open, cracked it open,
Cracked it open just now,
Oh, I just now cracked it open,
Cracked it open just now.

It was rotten...
Ate it anyway...
Got a stomachache...
Called the doctor...
Felt better...
Found a peanut...

Peanut Sitting on a Railroad Track (Tune: Polly Wolly Doodle)

A peanut sat on a railroad track,
His heart was all a-flutter.
Then round the bend came a railroad train.
Toot! Toot! Peanut butter!
Squish!

Literacy Activities

(Select one or two follow-up activities to do each time you sing a song or say a rhyme.)

Oral Language Development

1. Discuss peanut butter with the children. *How many of you like peanut butter? Do you like peanut butter sandwiches? What kind of jelly do you like on your sandwich?*

Comprehension

1. Ask the children why they think the last verse of the song is hummed.
2. Ask them if they can guess why some people name their small dogs "Peanut" or use the word as a nickname for young children.

Print Awareness

1. Challenge the children to brainstorm a list of things that have peanut butter in them, such as candy, cookies, pies, cakes, and so on. Ask them which of these things they have eaten before. *Which thing on the list do you like best?* Say the letters of each item as you add it to the list.

Learning Centers

Caution: Before attempting any of the activities be certain that no child has a sensitivity or allergy to peanuts.

Games (Peanut Roll)

Make two lines of masking tape down the length of a table. Encourage two children to race a peanut down the line by slightly nudging it with their finger. *What happens if you nudge too hard?*

Gross Motor (Peanut Toss)

Provide a contact paper-covered coffee can and some peanuts. Encourage the children to stand behind a throw line and attempt to toss the peanuts into the can.

Math (Match My Length)

Give each child an unshelled peanut. Challenge them to find something in the Math Center that is the same length as their peanut.

Writing (I Can Spell "Peanut")

Write the word "peanut" on an index card. Encourage the children to use the magnetic letters to copy the word. Some children will be able to write the word. Suggest that they write the word on an index card and add it to their Word Box (shoebox collection of words they can write).

Outdoor Play or Music and Movement Activity

1. Play Drop the Peanut as you would play Drop the Handkerchief. Choose one child to be IT while the other children sit in a circle facing the center. The child who is IT skips or walks around the outside of the circle and casually drops a peanut behind one of the children sitting in the circle. This child picks up the peanut and chases IT around the circle. IT tries to run around the circle and sit in the second child's spot without being tagged. If IT is not tagged, then he sits in his new spot in the circle and the child with the peanut is now IT. If IT is tagged, then he is IT for another round.

2. Sing along with "Peanut Butter" (*Where Is Thumbkin?* CD, Thomas Moore), "We Love Peanut Butter" (*Keep on Singing and Dancing* CD, Jean Feldman), "Make Myself Some Cookies" (*I Am Special* CD, Thomas Moore), or "Peanut Sitting on a Railroad Track" (*Silly Songs* CD, Disney).

BRAIN CONNECTION

Peanut butter is high in protein and is therefore considered a good brain food.

REFLECTIONS

Describe how you make a peanut butter and jelly sandwich.

Where do peanuts grow?

Raindrop Song

Raindrop Song
(Tune: Traditional)

If all the raindrops (wiggle fingers in the air)
Were lemon drops and gumdrops (tap one index finger against palm of
  other hand)
Oh, what a rain that would be! (wiggle fingers in the air)
Standing outside, with my mouth open wide.
Ah-ah-ah-ah-ah-ah-ah-ah-ah-ah! (stand, looking up with mouth open)
If all the raindrops
Were lemon drops and gumdrops,
Oh, what a rain that would be!

If all the snowflakes (repeat actions as above)
Were candy bars and milkshakes,
Oh, what a snow that would be!
Standing outside, with my mouth open wide.
Ah-ah-ah-ah-ah-ah-ah-ah-ah-ah!
If all the snowflakes
Were candy bars and milkshakes,
Oh, what a snow that would be!

If all the sunbeams
Were bubble gum and ice cream,
Oh, what a sun that would be!
Standing outside, with my mouth open wide.
Ah-ah-ah-ah-ah-ah-ah-ah-ah-ah!
If all the sunbeams
Were bubble gum and ice cream,
Oh, what a sun that would be!

THEME CONNECTIONS
Clothing
Food
Humor
Naptime/Sleeping
Real and Make-
 Believe
Seasons
Things I Like/
 Favorite Things
Time of Day
Weather

Related Songs, Chants, and Rhymes

Cap, Mittens, Shoes, and Socks
(Tune: Head, Shoulder, Knees, and Toes)

Cap, mittens, shoes, and socks,
Shoes and socks.
Cap, mittens, shoes, and socks,
Shoes and socks.
And pants and belt, and shirt and tie
Go together wet or dry
Wet or dry!

SEE ALSO
"The Ants Go
    Marching" p. 20
"Itsy Bitsy Spider"
    p. 130
"A Thunderstorm"
    p. 215
"The Weather
    Song" p. 214

It's Raining

It's raining, it's pouring,
The old man is snoring,
He went to bed and and he bumped
    his head
And he couldn't get up in the morning.

The Rain

Splish, splash,
Splish, splash,
Drip, drop,
Drip, drop,
Will the rain ever stop?

Rain, Rain, Go Away

Rain, rain, go away.
Come again another day

Rain, rain, go away.
Little children want to play.

Clouds, clouds, go away
Little children want to play.

Thunder, thunder, go away
Little children want to play

Rain, rain, come back soon.
Little flowers want to bloom.

Literacy Activities

(Select one or two follow-up activities to do each time you sing a song or say a rhyme.)

Oral Language Development

1. Discuss experiences children have had in the rain. *Have you ever been caught in the rain without an umbrella? How did the rain feel? What do you think it would feel like if the raindrops were hard candy lemon drops instead of water?*

Print Awareness

1. Print the song on chart paper. Sing the song once without the chart and then a second time, pointing out the left-to-right and top-to-bottom directions as you read.

Letter Knowledge and Recognition

1. Write "raindrop," "gumdrop," and "lemon drop" on chart paper. Ask the children which letters in each word are the same. Say the words. Write "drop" on the chart paper. Explain that this combination of letters will always spell "drop" and that when these letters come together in a word, you can hear each one. Read the words again.

Learning Centers

Art (It's Raining Candy)

Provide a variety of colors of paint. Encourage the children to paint pictures of lemon drops and gumdrops falling from the sky. Suggest that they add their favorite candy to the rainfall.

Discovery (Raindrop Art)

Put several colors of dry tempera paint in salt shakers and encourage the children to sprinkle it randomly on a sheet of paper. When they are finished, ask them to spray their picture using a spray bottle of water. *What happens?*

Science (The Sounds of Rain)

Give the children a spray bottle of water with an adjustable nozzle and a cookie sheet. Encourage them to spray their pretend rain on the cookie sheet using the nozzle to change the force of the water. Encourage them to describe the differences in sounds the water (raindrops) makes as it hits the cookie sheet.

Writing (What to Do on a Rainy Day)

Invite the children to tell a story or dictate a list of things about what they might do on a rainy day.

Outdoor Play or Music and Movement Activity

1. Play classical music with a variety of tempos. Invite the children to dance like different types of rain (e.g., slow, fast, hard, and drizzle).
2. Sing along with the "Raindrop Song" (*Where Is Thumbkin?* CD, Kimbo) or "My Umbrella" (*I Am Special* CD, Thomas Moore).

BRAIN CONNECTION

Rainy weather helps clean the air. A person generally feels fresh, inspired, and/or energized immediately following a rainfall because rain helps balance the electrical charges in the air.

REFLECTIONS

If candy fell from the sky when it rained, what kind of candy would you want to fall?

What do you like to do on a rainy day?

Rhyme Time

Rhyme Time
(Tune: The Addams Family)

Rhyme time, rhyme time,
Rhyme time, rhyme time, rhyme time.

There's can and there's pan,
There's fan and there's ran.
There's man and there's tan.
The "an" family.

"et" family—pet, jet, vet, net, let, set...
"ike" family—like, hike, bike, mike, trike, pike...
"ot" family—pot, dot, hot, not, lot, got...
"all" family—ball, call, hall, fall, tall, mall...
"it" family—sit, lit, hit, kit, fit, pit...
"ook" family—book, look, cook, hook, took, nook...

Related Songs, Chants, and Rhymes

Say and Touch

Say "red," and touch your head.
Say "sky," and touch your eye.
Say "bear," and touch your hair.
Say "hear," and touch your ear.
Say "south," and touch your mouth.
Say "rose," and touch your nose.

Say "in," and touch your chin.
Say "rest," and touch your chest.
Say "farm," and touch your arm.
Say "yummy," and touch your tummy.
Say "bee," and touch your knee.
Say "neat," and touch your feet.

Literacy Activities

(Select one or two follow-up activities to do each time you sing a song or say a rhyme.)

Oral Language Development

1. Ask the children if they know why rhyming words that are grouped together are called a "family." Write one set of words on the board and encourage the children to identify the common letters in the words. Explain that they all go together because of their common letters—like families are sometimes grouped by their last name. A family's last name is usually common to each member of the family.

THEME CONNECTIONS
Families
Parts of the Body
Sounds and
    Movement

SEE ALSO
"Down by the Bay"
p. 55

Phonological Awareness

1. Write each set of rhyming words on chart paper and encourage the children to identify the common letters. Does anyone have a name that rhymes with any of the sets?
2. Play the name game with the children. Make a rhyme with each child's name, for example, Madison, addison, rattison, battison.
3. Place a sock, a lock, a rock, and a clock in front of you. Invite the children to make up a story using the rhyming items.

Learning Centers

Games (Babble Scrabble)

Give the children scrabble letters. Encourage them to put letters together to make words.

Gross Motor (Eight Skate)

Use masking tape to make a numeral eight (8) on the floor. Ask the children to remove their shoes and "skate" the eight in their socks.

Language (Rhyme Time Hunt)

Hide rhyming items (can/pan, rock/sock, phone/bone, and so forth) in the center and encourage the children to find the items and place them in rhyming pairs.

Writing (Pink Ink)

Give the children pink felt markers and invite them to write with pink ink.

Outdoor Play or Music and Movement Activity

1. Play Don't Let the Ball Fall. Invite the children to toss a ball into the air and then try to keep it in the air.
2. Play Bubble Trouble. Blow bubbles and have the children think of way to keep the bubbles aloft.
3. Sing along with "Rhyme Time" (*Sing to Learn with Dr. Jean,* Jean Feldman) or "What's Your Name?" (*Silly Songs* CD, Disney).

REFLECTIONS

Which activity was your favorite activity today?

If we played a game with fish that had something to do with trying to get something that we wanted, what rhyming name could we call the game? (Fish Wish) (Think of other examples.)

Row, Row, Row Your Boat

Row, Row, Row Your Boat
(Tune: Traditional)

Row, row, row your boat
Gently down the stream.
Merrily, merrily, merrily, merrily,
Life is but a dream.

Related Songs, Chants, and Rhymes

Barges (Tune: Traditional)

Out of my window, looking in the night
I can see the barges' flickering light.
Silently flows the river to the sea,
And the barges too go silently.

Chorus:
Barges, I would like to go with you.
I would like to sail the ocean blue.
Barges, have you treasures in your hold?
Do you fight with pirates brave and bold?

Out of my window, looking in the night
I can see the barges' flickering light.
Starboard shines green and port is glowing red
I can see the barges far ahead.

Chorus

THEME CONNECTIONS

Boats and Ships
Emotions
Families
Oceans
Opposites
Rivers
Travel/Transportation
Weather

SEE ALSO

"There's a Hole in
   the Middle of
   the Sea" p. 190
"Wynken, Blynken,
   and Nod"
   p. 108

A Boy and a Girl in a Little Canoe (Tune: Traditional)

Just a boy and a girl in a little canoe
With the moon shining all around.
As he glides his paddle
You couldn't even hear a sound.

So they talked and they talked
Till the moon grew dim.
He said you better kiss me
Or get out and swim.

So whatcha gonna do in a little canoe
With the moon shinin' all a—
Boats goin' all a—
Girls swimmin' all a rou-ou-ound?

Motorboat, Motorboat

(suit actions to words)
Motorboat, motorboat, go so slow
Motorboat, motorboat go so fast (speed up a little)
Motorboat, motorboat step on the gas! (run)
Vroom!

My Bonnie Lies Over the Ocean (Tune: Traditional)

My Bonnie lies over the ocean,
My Bonnie lies over the sea.
My Bonnie lies over the ocean,
Please bring back my Bonnie to me.

Bring back,
Bring back,
Oh, bring back my Bonnie to me, to me.
Bring back,
Bring back,
Oh, bring back my Bonnie to me.

A Sailor Went to Sea (Tune: Traditional)

A sailor went to sea, sea, sea.
To see what she could see, see, see.
But all that she could see, see, see.
Was the bottom of the deep blue sea, sea, sea.

Literacy Activities

(Select one or two follow-up activities to do each time you sing a song or say a rhyme.)

Oral Language Development

1. Discuss the term "merrily." *What does it mean?* Try singing the song again, substituting the word "happily" for "merrily."
2. Discuss the word "gently." Ask a volunteer to demonstrate touching someone's hand gently. Sing the song again, substituting "quickly" for "gently." *If you change the word "quickly" for "gently," will it change the pace of the song?* Try singing the song more quickly.
3. Discuss experiences children may have had on a boat.
4. If available, show the children photos of different types of boats to stimulate discussion.

Learning Centers

Construction (Boat Building)

Give each child 12 craft sticks. Place 10 sticks horizontally and two sticks vertically at opposite ends, lying on top of the horizontal ones. Spread lots of glue on the sticks and let them dry. Use paint to decorate the "boats" when they are dry.

Fine Motor (Gentle Pick Up)

Give the children six plastic straws that have been cut in half. Encourage them to drop the straws in a pile and then pick them up, one at a time, trying not to move the other sticks. Play this like you would play Pick Up Sticks.

Games (Motorboat)

Play Motorboat, Motorboat. Children hold hands and move in a circle. They begin by moving slowly and then pick up the pace, going faster and faster as they recite the rhyme, "Motorboat, Motorboat" (see Related Songs, Chants, and Rhymes).

Writing (Waves)

Make Gel Bags by filling a zipper-closure plastic bag with ½ cup blue hair gel. Glue it shut. Show the children how to use their fingers to make "waves" (connected w's).

Outdoor Play or Music and Movement Activity

1. Try some of these music and movement ideas:
    -   Dance with scarves to "My Bonnie Lies Over the Ocean" (*Musical Scarves & Activities* CD, Kimbo).
    -   Sing along with "Row, Row, Row, Your Boat" (*Three Little Kittens* CD, Kimbo), "Row, Row, Row Your Boat" (*Walt Disney Records: Children's Favorite Songs Vol. 1* CD), or "Sailing Medley" (*Walt Disney Records: Children's Favorite Songs Vol. 2* CD).

REFLECTIONS

What is the difference in a boat and a ship?

If you could go somewhere on a ship where would you go?

Sing a Song of Opposites

Sing a Song of Opposites
by Pam Schiller
(Tune: Mary Had a Little Lamb)

This is big and this is small,
This is big; this is small,
This is big and this is small,
Sing along with me.

Other verse possibilities:
This is tall and this is short…
This is up and this is down…
This is in and this is out…
This is happy and this is sad…
This is soft and this is hard…
This is fast and this is slow…
This is here and this is there…

Related Songs, Chants, and Rhymes

High and Low

I reach my hands way up high. (reach high)
I can almost touch the sky.
Then I bend way down low (touch the floor)
And touch the floor just so.

Jack-in-the-Box (oh, so still)

Jack-in-the-box (tuck thumb into fist)
Oh, so still.
Won't you come out? (raise hand slightly)
Yes, I will. (pop thumb out of fist)

THEME CONNECTIONS

Movement
Opposites
Self-esteem
Spatial
    Relationships
Toys

Sometimes

Sometimes I am tall, (stand tall)

Sometimes I am small. (crouch low)

Sometimes I am very, very, tall. (stand on tiptoes)

Sometimes I am very, very small. (crouch and lower head)

Sometimes tall, (stand tall)

Sometimes small, (crouch down)

Sometimes neither tall or small. (stand normally)

Teddy Bear Opposites by Pam Schiller

(Suit actions to words)

Teddy Bear, Teddy Bear, stand up tall.

Teddy Bear, Teddy Bear, make yourself small.

Teddy Bear, Teddy Bear, step to the left.

Teddy Bear, Teddy Bear, step to the right.

Teddy Bear, Teddy Bear, run in place.

Teddy Bear, Teddy Bear, stand real still.

Teddy Bear, Teddy Bear, hold your hands up

Teddy Bear, Teddy Bear, put your hands down.

Teddy Bear, Teddy Bear, lay on your back.

Teddy Bear, Teddy Bear, roll to your front.

Teddy Bear, Teddy Bear, smile a smile.

Teddy Bear, Teddy Bear, look real sad.

Teddy Bear, Teddy Bear, stand up again.

Teddy Bear, Teddy Bear, sit right down.

Teddy Bear, Teddy Bear, go to sleep.

Teddy Bear, Teddy Bear, what's the opposite of sleep?

SEE ALSO

"Catalina
  Magnalina"
  p. 35

"The Grand Old
  Duke of York"
  p. 81

"Open, Shut Them"
  p. 160

Literacy Activities

(Select one or two follow-up activities to do each time you sing a song or say a rhyme.)

Oral Language Development

1. Discuss the pairs of opposites mentioned in the song. Challenge the children to add new verses.

Print Awareness

1. Challenge the children to look around the room for examples of opposites. Make a list of the pairs that they find.

Learning Centers

Art (Wide and Narrow)

Provide tempera paint and wide and narrow brushes. Invite the children to paint wide and narrow lines. Provide paint that is thick and thin and invite the children to explore each type of paint. Ask questions. *Is it easier to paint with thick or thin paint? What happens when the paint is thin?*

Discovery (Opposites)

Give the children a basket of items that represent pairs of opposites. For example, you might have things that are rough and smooth, thick and thin, and big and little. Encourage the children to pair the items.

Gross Motor (Over and Under)

Encourage the children to toss beanbags into a box using overhand throws and underhand throws. *Which is easier to do?*

Snack (Opposite Edibles)

Provide skinny and fat pretzels, small and large marshmallows, and soft and hard cookies for the children to sample. Talk with them as they eat the snacks. Ask them to name the opposite pairs.

Outdoor Play or Music and Movement Activity

1. Invite the children to dance to music with tempos that are slow and fast. *How does the tempo change the dance?*
2. Sing along with "High Low" (*I Am Special* CD, Thomas Moore) or "The Opposite Song" (*Keep on Singing and Dancing* CD, Jean Feldman).

BRAIN CONNECTION

Intelligence is, in large part, a person's ability to see patterns and build on those patterns. Patterns are made of likenesses and differences. The concept of opposites provides a great opportunity for children to see and understand extreme likenesses and differences.

REFLECTIONS

Can you think of some opposites you can show me with your thumb? (For example, pointing up and down, placing inside and outside fist, placing on and off knee, bent and straight, and so on.)

Skidamarink

Skidamarink
(Tune: Traditional)

Skidamarink a dink a dink,
Skidamarink a doo,
I love you.
Skidamarink a dink a dink,
Skidamarink a doo,
I love you.

I love you in the morning
And in the afternoon,
I love you in the evening
And underneath the moon;
Oh, Skidamarink a dink a dink,
Skidamarink a doo,
I love you!

Related Songs, Chants, and Rhymes

A Bicycle Built for Two (Tune: Traditional)

Daisy, Daisy, give me your answer true.
I'm half crazy all for the love of you.
It won't be a stylish marriage.
I can't afford a carriage.
But you'll look sweet, upon the seat
Of a bicycle built for two.

A Tisket, A Tasket (Tune: Traditional)

A tisket, a tasket,
A green and yellow basket,
I wrote a letter to my love
And on the way I lost it.

THEME CONNECTIONS

Colors
Emotions
Families
Friends
Numbers
Sun, Moon, Stars
Time of Day
Travel/Transportation

SEE ALSO

"Frog Went A-
    Courtin'" p. 70
"Lavender's Blue"
    p. 127
"Mr. Sun" p. 146
"My Bonnie Lies
    Over the
    Ocean" p. 176

I lost it, I lost it,
And on the way I lost it.
A little boy, he picked it up,
And put it in his pocket.

His pocket, his pocket,
He put it in his pocket.
A little boy, he picked it up,
And put it in his pocket.

Literacy Activities

(Select one or two follow-up activities to do each time you sing a song or say a rhyme.)

Oral Language Development

1. Teach the children how to sign, "I love you" (appendix p. 240).

Comprehension

1. Ask children questions about the song. *What is the song, "Skidamarink" about?*

Letter Knowledge and Recognition

1. Write the word "skidamarink" on chart paper. Ask the children to identify the letters that they recognize.
2. Print the phrase, "I love you" on chart paper. Show the children how to write "I love you" using the letter I, a heart, and the letter U.

Print Awareness

1. Print the song on chart paper. Sing the song, pointing out the left-to-right and top-to-bottom progression of the words.

Learning Centers

Art (Someone Special)

Have the children draw a picture of someone who is special to them. Encourage them to dictate a sentence about what they like about the special person.

Language ("Dink" and "Do" Rhyme)

Provide a box of objects that rhyme with "dink" and "do" (e.g., pink marker, blue marker, numeral 2, ink, shoe, glue, and a learning link). Write the words "dink" and "do" on sheets of construction paper. Have the children sort the items according to the word with which they rhyme.

Science (Heartbeat)

Provide a stethoscope. Encourage the children to listen to each other's heartbeats. Have them stand and do some exercises. *What happens to your heartbeat after you exercise?*

Writing (I Love You)

Write, "I love you" on chart paper. Also write the shortened form of "I love you" (the letter I, a heart, and the letter U). Encourage the children to copy the phrase both ways. *Which way is easier?* Some children will be able to write the words. Suggest that they write the words on index cards and add them to their Word Box (shoebox collection of words they can write).

Outdoor Play or Music and Movement Activity

1. Play Drop the Heart as you would Drop the Handkerchief. Choose one child to be IT while the other children sit in a circle facing the center. The child who is IT skips or walks around the outside of the circle and casually drops a paper heart behind one of the children sitting in the circle. This child picks up the heart and chases IT around the circle. IT tries to run around the circle and sit in the second child's spot without being tagged. If IT is not tagged, then he sits in his new spot in the circle and the child with the heart is now IT. If IT is tagged, then he is IT for another round.

2. Sing along with "A Tisket, A Tasket" (*Three Little Kittens* CD, Kimbo), "A Bicycle Built for Two" (*Walt Disney Favorites Vol. 1* CD), or "A Tisket, A Tasket" (*Playtime Favorites* CD, Music Little People).

BRAIN CONNECTION

We associate love with our heart, for example, "I love you with all my heart," "My heart is broken," "I give you my heart," and so forth. The truth is, all emotions are controlled by the brain. It is just not as romantic to say, "I love you with all my head."

REFLECTIONS

Who would you sing "Skidamarink" to? Who would sing it to you?

Whose picture did you draw in the Art Center? Why did you choose that person?

Take Me Out to the Ball Game

Take Me Out to the Ball Game
(Tune: Traditional)

Take me out to the ball game
Take me out with the crowd.
Buy me some peanuts and crackerjack,
I don't care if I ever get back,
So it's root, root, root for the home team,
If they don't win it's a shame
For it's one, two, three strikes
You're out! at the old ball game.

Related Songs, Chants, and Rhymes

All Through the Game by Pam Schiller
(Tune: The Wheels on the Bus)

The pitcher on the mound throws the ball
Throws the ball, throws the ball.
The pitcher on the mound throws the ball,
All through the game.

The batter at home plate swings the bat,
Swings the bat, swings the bat.
The batter at home plate swings the bat,
All through the game.

The fans in the stands say, "He was safe."
"He was safe." "He was safe."
The fans in the stands say, "He was safe."
All through the game.

The coach on the bench says, "Good job, kids!"
"Good job, boys!" "Good job, kids!"
The coach on the bench says, "Good job, kids!"
At the end of the game.

Literacy Activities

(Select one or two follow-up activities to do each time you sing a song or say a rhyme.)

Oral Language Development

1. Discuss the game of baseball with the children. Ask questions to determine how much they know about the game. *Has anyone been to a baseball game? Does anyone play baseball? Who is your favorite team?* Talk about some of the terms used in baseball, such as "ball park," "ball field," "infield," "outfield," "bases," "homeruns," "dugout," "teams," "umpire," and so forth.

THEME
CONNECTIONS
Things I Like/
    Favorite Things
Things That Go
    Together

SEE ALSO
"I Can, You Can!"
    p. 153
"These Little Hands
    of Mine" p. 161

2. Discuss the vocabulary in the song that may be new to the children (e.g., "crackerjacks," "home team," "root," and "strike").

Letter Knowledge and Recognition

1. Write the word "ball" on chart paper. Discuss each letter in the word. *Which letter is written twice?* Write the word "baseball" on the chart. Ask a volunteer to point to the part of the word that spells "ball." Tell the children that the word baseball is made up of two words—"base" and "ball." Write each word separately.

Learning Centers

Blocks (Baseball Diamonds)

Give the children a large square of green felt to use as a baseball diamond and some small, brown felt squares to use as bases. Encourage them to create a ball field with the felt and use blocks to build the bleachers around the field.

Dramatic Play (Ball Hats)

Place as many baseball hats as you can gather in the center. Encourage the children to try them on. *Can you tell which team's hat you are wearing? How do you know?*

Gross Motor (Ball Roll)

Provide baseballs and clean, empty ice cream cartons. Lay the ice cream cartons on their sides and make a start line with masking tape about 3' from the cartons. Encourage the children to roll the baseballs into the cartons.

Writing (Baseball)

Cut a baseball shape from white poster board. Draw a line down the center of the "baseball." Then draw a line down the center of each of the two halves, dividing the ball into fourths. Write the word "ball" on the baseball, placing one letter in each segment. Now cut the sections apart and challenge the children to put the letters back together to spell "ball." Of course, this is a self-checking activity because if they put the letters in the correct sequence, they will have a baseball.

Outdoor Play or Music and Movement Activity

1. Provide empty paper towel tubes for bats and wadded paper for balls. Encourage the children to bat the balls.
2. Try some of these music and movement ideas:
   - 🎵 Dance with scarves to "Take Me Out to the Ball Game" (*Musical Scarves & Activities* CD).
   - 🎵 Sing along with "Paper Towel Tube" (*My Magical World* CD, Thomas Moore) or "Take Me Out to the Ball Game" (*Walt Disney Records: Children's Favorite Songs Vol. 1* CD).

REFLECTIONS

Have you ever been to a game? Have you ever seen a game on TV?

Can you throw a ball or hit a ball better?

Ten in the Bed

Ten in the Bed
(Tune: Traditional)

There were ten in the bed (hold up ten fingers)
And the little one said,

> *"Roll over! Roll over!"* (roll hand over hand)
> *So they all rolled over*
> *And one rolled out.* (hold up one finger)

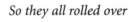

> *There were nine in the bed. . .* (repeat hand motions)
> *. . .eight in the bed. . .*
> *. . .seven in the bed. . .*
> *. . .six in the bed. . .*
> *. . .five in the bed. . .*
> *. . .four in the bed. . .*
> *. . .three in the bed. . .*
. . .two in the bed. . .

There was one in the bed
And the little one said,
"Alone at last!" (place head on hands as if sleeping)

(To shorten the song, change the song to "Five in the Bed.")

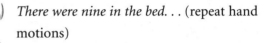

Related Songs, Chants, and Rhymes

Five Little Monkeys

Five little monkeys jumping on the bed.
One fell off and bumped her head.
Mama called the doctor, and the doctor said,
"No more monkeys jumping on the bed!"

(Repeat, subtracting a monkey each time. Say the rhyme using fingers or let children act it out.)

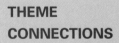

There Was an Old Woman Who Lived in a Shoe by Pam Schiller

There was an old woman who lived in a shoe.
She had so many children she didn't know what to do.
She gave them some playdough, puzzles and glue
And she added a playroom to the toe of her shoe.

SEE ALSO
"Are You Sleeping?"
p. 26
"Hush, Little Baby"
p. 107
"Rockabye, Baby"
p. 107

Literacy Activities

(Select one or two follow-up activities to do each time you sing a song or say a rhyme.)

Comprehension

1. Ask the children why the little one keeps saying, "Roll over." *Have you ever slept in a bed with other people? What was it like? Did you feel crowded? Did you have enough covers?*

2. Encourage the children to dramatize the story, "The Princess and the Pea." Use a marble as the pea and provide several pillows for mattresses. Ask questions when the story is over. *What problem did the princess have while she was trying to sleep? What problem did the little one in "Ten in the Bed" have while trying to sleep? Which one do you think slept the best?*

Phonological Awareness

1. Encourage the children to think of sounds people make when they sleep, such as snoring, deep breathing, little moans, and so on. Let the children demonstrate snoring sounds. *Are any of the sounds **onomatopoeic** sounds?*

2. Invite the children to brainstorm words that rhyme with "ten."

Letter Knowledge and Recognition

1. Write the letter "z" several times on a piece of chart paper (zzzzzz). Explain that z's are often used to represent the sounds people make when they sleep.

Learning Centers

Art (Roller Art)

Give the children paint rollers (the smaller the better) and encourage them to paint a picture with them. Call attention to the "rolling over" action of the roller.

Blocks (Build a Bed)

Encourage the children to build a bed with blocks that would be big enough to accommodate 10 (or five) children. Ask questions. *How will you know when the bed is big enough? What can you use to make their bed softer?*

Gross Motor (Roly Poly Races)

Use colored (red, yellow, blue, and green) vinyl tape to make four, 10' lines on the floor. Space the lines about 3' apart. Cover empty toilet paper tubes with construction paper to make "roly polys" to match each color line. Invite four children to select a color line and then race the matching "roly poly" along that line by rolling it. Have them chant "roll over, roll over" as they race. If a "roly poly" gets off the line, the player must put it back on the line at the point where it fell off. The first child to reach the end of the line wins.

Writing (Roll Over)

Write the words "roll over" on large index cards. Provide a roller bottle (a clean, empty roll-on deodorant bottle) and encourage the children to trace the letters by rolling over them with paint.

Outdoor Play or Music and Movement Activity

1. Cut a 10' sheet of butcher paper to represent a large bed. Have ten children lie on the bed and act out the song as it is sung. Be sure to establish which direction everyone will roll. *If everyone rolls to the left, who rolls out of the bed first? If everyone rolls to the right, who rolls out of the bed first?*
2. Sing along with "Roll Over" (*Where Is Thumbkin?* CD, Kimbo), "Five Little Monkeys" (*Dr. Jean and Friends* CD by Jean Feldman), "Five Little Monkeys" (*Hunk-Ta-Bunk-Ta Chants* CD, Hunk-Ta-Bunk-Ta Music), or "Ten in the Bed" (*Playtime Favorites* CD, Music Little People).

There's a Hole in the Bucket

There's a Hole in the Bucket
(Tune: Traditional)

There's a hole in the bucket,
Dear Liza, dear Liza.
There's a hole in the bucket,
Dear Liza, there's a hole.

Then fix it, dear Henry,
Dear Henry, dear Henry.
Then fix it, dear Henry,
Dear Henry, fix it.

With what shall I fix it? Dear Liza…
With a straw, dear Henry...
But the straw is too long, dear Liza…
Then cut it, dear Henry...
With what shall I cut it? Dear Liza…
With an axe, dear Henry...
The axe is too dull, dear Liza…
Then sharpen it, dear Henry...
With what shall I sharpen it? Dear Liza…
With a stone, dear Henry...
The stone is too dry, dear Liza…
Then whet it, dear Henry...
With what shall I whet it? Dear Liza...
With water, dear Henry...
How shall I get it? Dear Liza...
In the bucket, dear Henry...
There's a hole in the bucket, dear Liza...

THEME CONNECTIONS
Animals
Families
Friends
Houses and Homes
Humor
Opposites
Problem Solving
Spatial
    Relationships
Work

Related Songs, Chants, and Rhymes

Jack and Jill
Jack and Jill went up the hill
To fetch a pail of water.
Jack fell down

And broke his crown
And Jill came tumbling after.

There's a Hole in the Middle of the Sea (Tune: Traditional)

There's a hole in the middle of the sea,
There's a hole in the middle of the sea,
There's a hole, there's a hole,
There's a hole in the middle of the sea.

There's a log in the hole in the middle of the sea.
There's a log in the hole in the middle of the sea.
There's a log, there's a log,
There's a log in the hole in the middle of the sea.

There's a bump on the log in the hole in the middle of the sea...
There's a frog on the bump on the log in the hole in the middle of the sea...
There's a fly on the frog on the bump on the log in the hole in the middle of the sea...
There's a wing on the fly on the frog on the bump on the log in the hole in the middle
    of the sea...
There's a flea on the wing on the fly on the frog on the bump on the log in the hole in
    the middle of the sea...

Literacy Activities

(Select one or two follow-up activities to do each time you sing a song or say a rhyme.)

Comprehension

1. "There's a Hole in the Bucket" is structured around two easy-to-identify patterns. The first pattern is question/answer; the second pattern is a circular pattern because the song ends right where it started. Call children's attention to these two patterns. Ask them to think of other songs or chants that have a question/answer format. ("Where Is Thumbkin?") Ask the children if they can remember any other songs or chants that are circular ("Michael Finnegan" and "One, Two Buckle My Shoe").

Oral Language Development

1. Challenge the children to think of other words for "bucket", such as "pail" or "container".

Learning Centers

Construction (Then Mend It)

Give the children a bucket (an empty gallon ice cream container) with a hole cut in the bottom. Provide some materials to fix the hole, such as tape, straw, sticks, playdough, clay, and paper. Challenge the children to mend the hole.

Discovery (Can You Solve This?)

Give the children a bowl filled with birdseed, sand, and gravel. Provide three smaller containers, a strainer, and a colander. Place all the materials over a tray to avoid as much mess as possible. Ask them to separate the three items so they can feed the birdseed to the birds.

Language (A Circular Story)

Give the children a bucket, a straw, a plastic knife, a stone, and an empty cup of water. Ask the children to sequence the items in the order they are presented in the story. What happens when they get to the water in the sequence and need a bucket? After they have laid the items in a line, have them arrange the items in a circle.

Writing (Dear)

Write the word "dear" on index cards. Have the children use magnetic letters to copy the word. Explain that the word "dear" is often used to address someone in a letter. Some children will be able to write the word. Suggest that they write the word on an index card and add it to their Word Box (shoebox collection of words they can write).

Outdoor Play or Music and Movement Activity

1. Show the children how to form a water brigade. Ask them to line up in a straight line. Place a large bucket at the end of the line. Pass one cup of water down the line, child to child, until it arrives to the last child. Have the last child pour the water in the bucket. Continue until the bucket is full.

2. Sing along with "There's a Hole in the Bucket" (*Three Little Kittens* CD, Kimbo), "There's a Hole in My Bucket" (*Walt Disney Records: Children's Favorite Songs Vol. 4* CD), or "There's a Hole in the Middle of the Sea" (*Silly Songs* CD, Disney).

BRAIN CONNECTION

The brain forges wiring connections for problem solving abilities during the first four years of life. Connections are made as children experience solving problems. The more experiences children have, the stronger the wiring becomes. Strong wiring means faster responses when a problem arises.

REFLECTIONS

Have you ever had something that needed mending? What was it? How did you get it mended?

For what activities do we use buckets and pails?

This Little Light of Mine

This Little Light of Mine
(Tune: Traditional)

This little light of mine,
I'm going to let it shine.
This little light of mine,
I'm going to let it shine,
This little light of mine,
I'm going to let it shine,
Let it shine, let shine, let it shine.

When I'm playing with my friends,
I'm going to let it shine.
When I'm playing with my friends,
I'm going to let it shine.
When I'm playing with my friends,
I'm going to let it shine.
Let it shine, let shine, let it shine.

When I'm singing at my school,
I'm going to let it shine.
When I'm singing at my school,
I'm going to let it shine.
When I'm singing at my school,
I'm going to let it shine.
Let it shine, let shine, let it shine.

*The second and third verses were adapted by Pam Schiller.
(Add your own verses that reflect activities that the children are involved in.)

THEME CONNECTIONS
Self
Self-Esteem
Things I Like/
    Favorite Things

Related Songs, Chants, and Rhymes

These Are Things I Like to Do by Pam Schiller (Tune: Mulberry Bush)

These are things I like to do,
Like to do, like to do.
These are things I like to do,
I know a trick or two.

This is the way I read a book, (suit actions to words)
Read a book, read a book.
This is the way I read a book,
I know a trick or two.

This is the way I paint a picture…
This is the way I ride my bike…
This is the way I work a puzzle...
This is the way I throw the ball...
This is the way I help my dad...
This is the way I climb a tree...

Uniquely Me by Pam Schiller

My mom says I'm uniquely me (point to self)
I look in the mirror 'cause I want to see. (hold palm up like a mirror)
Here are my eyes, nose, mouth, and hair (point to each body part)
But nothing I see appears to be rare. (shake head)

I look around at all my friends (look at friends)
And think about what makes them friends.
Then I know what I'm looking for (hold finger up like you just thought of something)
Unique is what makes you who you are.

It's what you say and what you do (turn right palm up, then left palm up)
That makes you uniquely you! (point to self)

Warm-Up Chant by Thomas Moore*

(children echo each phrase)
I love myself, I feel so good.
This is my nose; I smell with my nose.
I love my nose.

These are my ears, I wash my ears.
I hear with my ears; I have holes in my ears.
I love my ears.

These are my teeth, I brush my teeth.
I floss my teeth, I chew with my teeth.
I love my teeth.

This is my chin, my chinny-chin-chin.
I don't know why I have it. I love my chin.

*Singing, Moving, and Learning CD

SEE ALSO
"I Can, You Can!"
   p. 153
"I Have Something
   in My Pocket"
   p. 124
"If You're Happy
   and You Know
   It" p. 124
"Itsy Bitsy Spider"
   p. 130

This is my back, I scratch my back.
I dance with my back. I love my back.

This is my tummy, my yummy, yummy, tummy.
I put ice cream in my tummy…
…jelly beans…
…French fries…
…broccoli…
…potato chips
…hamburgers…
…pizza…
…tummy ache, my tummy ache…

This is me. I am special.
I love me, and I love you.

Literacy Activities

(Select one or two follow-up activities to do each time you sing a song or say a rhyme.)

Comprehension

1. Help the children understand the meaning of the words in the song. *What does it mean when we say, "This little light of mine, I'm gonna let it shine"?* Talk about doing your best and about being kind to others.

Print Awareness

1. Using the predictable text of the song, invite children to write a new verse. You may want to write most of the words on a chart and just leave a few blanks for the children to fill in. For example, "When I'm _____ with my friends…" or "When I'm _____ with my family."

Learning Centers

Art (My Best Painting)

Provide tempera paint and challenge the children to paint their very best painting. For added fun, paint with fluorescent paint under a black light.

Discovery (Light Sources)

Provide several sources of light, for example, a flashlight, lamp, candle, and nightlight. Encourage the children to discuss how each type of light is used.

Gross Motor (Shadow Play)

Provide a light source such as a flashlight or an overhead projector and some music. Encourage the children to dance between the light and the wall to create dancing shadows.

Writing (Things I'm Good At)

Invite the children to talk about things they feel they are good at. Make a list of their ideas and encourage them to add to their list.

Outdoor Play or Music and Movement Activity

1. Invite the children to play Flashlight Tag. One child holds the flashlight. He or she counts to 10 and the other children start to run. The flashlight holder attempts to touch a child with the light from the flashlight. If a child is touched, he or she becomes the holder of the flashlight and the game begins again.

2. Try these music and movement ideas:
   - Play rhythm band instruments to upbeat music.
   - Sing along with "I Like You, There's No Doubt About It" (*Dr. Jean Sings Silly Songs* CD, Jean Feldman) or "I Like You, I Like Me" (*I Am Special* CD, Thomas Moore).

REFLECTIONS

What is something that you are really good at?

How do you feel when you do something well?

This Little Piggy

This Little Piggy

This little piggy went to market,
    (wiggle big toe or thumb)
This little piggy stayed home,
        (wiggle second toe or index finger)
This little piggy had roast beef,
    (wiggle middle toe or finger)
This little piggy had none,
    (wiggle fourth toe or ring finger)
And this little piggy cried
    "Wee-wee-wee!" all the way home.
        (wiggle little toe or little finger)

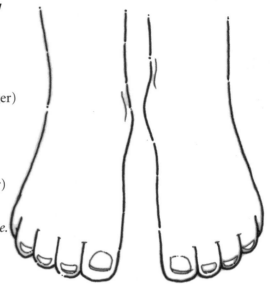

Related Songs, Chants, and Rhymes

To Market, to Market

To market, to market,
To buy a fat pig.
Home again, home again,
Jiggety-jig.

To market, to market,
To buy a fat hog.
Home again, home again,
Jiggety-jog.

Literacy Activities

(Select one or two follow-up activities to do each time you sing a song or say a rhyme.)

Oral Language Development

1. Show photos of pigs and hogs, if available. Use the photos to stimulate discussion. Point out the difference between hogs and pigs. (Hogs are larger than pigs.)

2. Ask the children to take off their shoes. Say "This Little Piggy" with them and have them use their toes as the piggies. *Why do we call toes "piggies"?* Ask a volunteer to say the names of some of the toes (big toe, middle toe, and little toe).

**THEME
CONNECTIONS**
Animals
Houses and Homes
Movement
Parts of the Body

3. Some children's programs and cartoons feature pigs. Ask the children to name some famous pigs, for example, Porky, Wilbur, and Piglet.

Phonological Awareness

1. Recite "To Market, To Market." Identify the rhyming words ("pig/jig" and "hog/jog"). *What is the difference between a pig and a hog?*

Learning Centers

Art (Piggy Prints)

Provide a shallow tray of paint and a 12' piece of butcher paper. Invite the children to remove their shoes and step into the paint. Have them walk the length of the butcher paper. Place a tub of soapy water and a towel at the end of the paper so they children can wash their feet. It's messy, but fun! Label the children's toes and write their name beside their footprint. Ask them to show you their big toe and their little toe on their footprint.

Blocks (Over the Stile)

Have the children build a stile (gate) with blocks and then pretend to be pigs jumping over it. *How would a pig jump? Is it easier for a child or a pig to jump over the fence? Why?*

Fine Motor (Piggy Pick Up)

Provide stringing beads in a box. Encourage the children to take off their shoes and try to pick up the beads with their toes. *Is this difficult? Would it be easier to use your hands?*

Writing (Wee, Wee, Wee)

Write the words "wee, wee, wee" on chart paper. Provide magnetic letters and invite the children to copy the words. *How many "e"'s do you need?*

Outdoor Play or Music and Movement Activity

1. Play Hog, Hog, Pig as you would Duck, Duck, Goose. Children sit in a circle. The child who is IT walks around the outside of the circle, tapping each player on the head and saying, "Hog." Eventually IT taps a player and says, "Pig" instead. The tapped player gets up and chases IT around the circle. If she taps IT before they get around the circle, she gets to go back to her place. If she doesn't, she becomes the new IT and the game continues.

SEE ALSO
"Down By the Bay"
    p. 55
"Old MacDonald
    Had a Farm"
    p. 156

REFLECTIONS

Which is bigger: a pig or a hog? A hog or a cow?

What color are pigs? Are they always pink?

This Old Man

This Old Man
(Tune: Traditional)

This old man, he played one. (hold up one finger)
He played knick-knack on my thumb. (knock on thumb)

Chorus:
With a knick-knack paddy whack give a dog a bone. (knock on head, clap twice,
   pretend to throw a bone over your shoulder)
This old man came rolling home. (roll hand over hand)

This old man, he played two. (hold up two fingers)
He played knick-knack on my shoe. (knock on shoe)

Chorus

This old man, he played three (hold up three fingers)
He played knick-knack on my knee. (knock on knee)

Chorus

This old man, he played four (hold up four fingers)
He played knick-knack on the door. (knock on door)

Chorus

This old man, he played five (hold up five fingers)
He played knick-knack on a hive. (knock on a hive)

Chorus

...six...sticks (continue hand motions)
...seven...heaven
...eight...gate
...nine...line
...ten...over again!

THEME CONNECTIONS

Counting/Numbers
Music
Sounds of Language
Things That Go
   Together

198

Related Songs, Chants, and Rhymes

Big Bass Drum

Oh! We can play on the big bass drum,
And this is the way we do it:
Rub-a-dub, boom, goes the big bass drum,
And this is the way we do it.

Oh! We can play on the violin,
And this is the way we do it:
Zum, zum, zin, says the violin,
Rub-a-dub, boom goes the big bass drum,
And this is the way we do it.

Oh! We can play on the little flute,
And this is the way we do it:
Tootle, toot, toot, says the little flute,
Zum, zum, zin, goes the violin
Rub-a-dub, boom goes the big bass
    drum.
And this is the way we do it.

SEE ALSO
"The Ants Go
    Marching" p. 20
"Old Mother
    Hubbard" p. 33

MacNamara's Band (Tune: Traditional)

My name is MacNamara,
I'm the leader of the band,
And though we're small in number,
We're the best in all the land.
Of course, I'm the conductor
And I've often had to play
With all the fine musicians
That you read about today.

Just now we are practicing
For a very grand affair,
It's an annual celebration,
All the gentry will be there.
The girls and boys will all turn out
With flags and colours grand,
And in front of the procession
Will be MacNamara's Band.

Chorus:
The drums they bang, the cymbals clang,
The horns they blaze away,
Macarthy puffs the ould bassoon,
Doyle and I the pipes do play.
Hennessey tuteily tootles the flute,
The music is something grand,
And a credit to ould Ireland's boys
Is MacNamara's Band.

Chorus

One, Two, Buckle My Shoe

One, two, buckle my shoe;
Three, four, shut the door;
Five, six, pick up sticks;
Seven, eight, lay them straight;
Nine, ten, a big fat hen.

This Old Man Is Rockin' On by Pam Schiller and Tracy Moncure (Tune: This Old Man)

This old man, he played drums.
With his fingers and his thumbs.

Chorus:
With a knick-knack paddy whack
    give a dog a bone.
This old man is rockin' on.

This old man, he played flute,
Made it hum and made it toot.

Chorus

This old man, he played strings,
Twangs and twops and zips and zings.

Chorus

This old man, he played bass,
With a big grin on his face.

Chorus

This old man, he played gong
At the end of every song.

Chorus

This old man, he could dance.
He could strut and he could prance.

Chorus

This old man was a band,
Very best band in the land.

Chorus

Literacy Activities

(Select one or two follow-up activities to do each time you sing a song or say a rhyme.)

Letter Knowledge and Recognition

1. Write "knick-knack" on chart paper. Have the children identify the letters that they know. *Which letters appear more than once? How many times do you see the letter "k"? How about "a"? How many letters are the same in each word? How many are different?*

Comprehension

1. The song is unclear as to what it means to play one, play two, and so forth. Ask the children what they think the words of the song mean. *What does it mean when the song says the old man played one? Played two? What did he play? An instrument? A game? How do you play one? How do you play knick-knack?*

Learning Centers

Blocks (Paddy Whack)

Make Paper Bag Blocks. Fill grocery sacks ¾ full with crumpled newspaper, fold the tops down, square them, and then tape them closed. Give the children the Paper Bag Blocks and an empty paper towel tube. Encourage them to play Paddy Whack by stacking the blocks and then knocking them down with the "paddy whacker" (empty paper towel tube).

Games (Rolling Home)

Build a home for the old man out of blocks or a large box. Draw an old man, color, and laminate him, if desired. Cover a one-pound coffee can with construction paper or contact paper and then glue the old man to the can. Use masking tape to make a start line about 6' from the old man's house. Challenge children to roll the old man from the start line to his house. If you make a large doorway, they can even try to roll him into his house.

Language (Rhyming Word Match)

Write the rhyming words from the song on index cards. Use markers or crayons to write each set of rhyming words in a different color. Have the children match the pairs of rhyming words.

Writing (Knick-Knack)

Write "knick-knack" on large index cards. Provide empty, clean roll-on deodorant bottles filled with tempera paint and invite the children to trace the letters, rolling the paint along the lines of the letters.

Outdoor Play or Music and Movement Activity

1. Use a marker to identify "home" and a second marker to identify a start line. Encourage the children to roll home using forward rolls or log rolls.
2. Sing along with "One, Two, Buckle My Shoe" (*Playtime Favorites* CD, Music Little People), "This Old Man" (*Here Is Thumbkin!* CD, Kimbo), or "This Old Man" (*For Our Children: 10th Anniversary Edition* CD, Rhino).

BRAIN CONNECTION
Both rocking and rolling will improve children's balance and coordination.

REFLECTIONS
How would the song be different if a cat was in the song instead of a dog? What would the old man throw to the cat?

Can you think of an insect that rhymes with three?

Three Bears Rap

Three Bears Rap

Shh, shh, shh, shh, shh, shh, shh,
 shh, shh, shh.
Out in the forest in a
 wee little cottage
 lived the three
 bears.
Shh, shh, shh, shh, shh,
 shh, shh, shh,
 shh, shh.
One was the Mama
 Bear, one was the Papa
 Bear, and one was the wee bear.
Shh, shh, shh, shh, shh, shh, shh, shh, shh, shh.

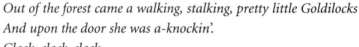

Out of the forest came a walking, stalking, pretty little Goldilocks
And upon the door she was a-knockin'.
Clack, clack, clack.
But no one was there, unh-unh, no one was there.
So she walked right in and had herself a bowl.
She didn't care, unh-unh, she didn't care.

Home, home, home came the three bears.

"Someone's been eating my porridge," said the Mama Bear.
"Someone's been eating my porridge," said the Papa Bear.
"Baa-baa Barebear," said the little Wee Bear.
"Someone's broken my chair."
Crash!

Just then Goldilocks woke up.
She broke up the party and she beat it out of there.

"Good-bye, good-bye, good-bye," said the Mama Bear.
"Good-bye, good-bye, good-bye," said the Papa Bear.
"Baa-baa Barebear," said the little Wee Bear.
That's the story of the three little bears—yeah!

THEME CONNECTIONS

Animals
Sizes
Traditional Tales

Related Songs, Chants, and Rhymes

Goldilocks, Goldilocks

Goldilocks, Goldilocks, turn around. (turn around)

Goldilocks, Goldilocks, touch the ground. (touch the ground)

Goldilocks, Goldilocks, knock on the door. (pretend to knock with your hand)

Goldilocks, Goldilocks, eat some porridge. (pretend to eat porridge)

Goldilocks, Goldilocks, have a seat. (squat)

Goldilocks, Goldilocks, go to sleep. (put head on folded hands)

Goldilocks, Goldilocks, run, run, run. (run in place)

SEE ALSO
"The Bear Went
Over the
Mountain"
p. 77
"Going on a Bear
Hunt" p. 76

There Once Were Three Brown Bears
(Tune: Twinkle, Twinkle, Little Star)

There once were three brown bears,
Mother, Father, Baby Bear.
Mother's food was way too cold.
Father's food was way too hot.
Baby's food was all gone.
Someone ate it, so he cried.

There once were three brown bears,
Mother, Father, Baby Bear.
Mother's chair was way too low.
Father's chair was way too high.
Baby's chair was just so right,
But when she sat, she broke it.

There once were three brown bears,
Mother, Father, Baby Bear.
Mother's bed was way too soft.
Father's bed was way too hard.
Baby's bed was occupied.
Someone strange was sleeping there.

"Come here quickly," Baby cried.
"Someone's sleeping in my bed!"
"Who are you?" asked Baby Bear.
"Who are you?" asked Goldilocks.
"You better run," said Baby Bear.
"I will!" said Goldilocks.

Literacy Activities

(Select one or two follow-up activities to do each time you sing a song or say a rhyme.)

Oral Language Development

1. Discuss the words that may be new vocabulary for the children, such as "cottage," "stalking," and "wee."

2. Because this is a rap it has some unusual phrases, for example, "beat it out of there," "baa-baa Barebear," and "had herself a bowl." Talk with the children about ways that a rap is different from a song and explain the unusual phrases.

Phonological Awareness

1. Discuss the sound effects in the rap ("crash," "clack," and "shh"). *Are they examples of onomatopoeia?*

Learning Centers

Construction (Goldilocks Puppets)

Give the children a 6" Styrofoam plate, a tongue depressor, wiggle eyes, and yellow paper ribbon. Invite the children to make a Goldilocks puppet by creating a face on the plate, adding hair (ribbon), and then gluing the face to the tongue depressor. Demonstrate how to use a plastic knife to pull the ribbon to make it curl. Encourage the children to talk for their puppets as you ask them questions. *What did you do when you went inside the bear's house? Which chair did you like best?*

Dramatic Play (Three Bear's Cottage)

Encourage the children to set up the Housekeeping Center as if it is the three bears' cottage.

Language (Goldilocks and the Bears)

Encourage the children to use puppets to retell and act out the story of "Goldilocks and Three Bears."

Writing (Dear Bears, I'm Sorry)

Invite the children to dictate a letter from Goldilocks to the three bears apologizing for entering their home without permission.

Outdoor Play or Music and Movement Activity

1. Sing along with "The Three Bears Rap" (*Here Is Thumbkin!* CD, Kimbo) or "The Three Boppin' Bears Rap" (*Dr. Jean Sings Silly Songs* CD, Jean Feldman).

REFLECTIONS

How is a rap like a song? How is it different?

How would the story be different if Goldilocks had not entered the house without permission?

Tiny Tim

Tiny Tim

I had a little turtle,
His name was Tiny Tim.
I put him in the bathtub,
To see if he could swim.

He drank up all the water,
He ate up all the soap,
Tiny Tim was choking
On the bubbles in his throat.

In came the doctor,
In came the nurse,
In came the lady,
With the alligator purse.

They pumped out all the water,
They pumped out all the soap
They popped the airy bubbles
As they floated from his throat.

Out went the doctor,
Out went the nurse,
Out went the lady,
With the alligator purse.

THEME CONNECTIONS
Amphibians
Animals
Humor
Nature
Occupations
Spatial
   Relationships

Related Songs, Chants, and Rhymes

There Once Was a Turtle

There was a little turtle. (make a fist)
He lived in a box. (draw a square in the air)
He swam in a puddle. (pretend to swim)
He climbed on the rocks. (pretend to climb)
He snapped at a mosquito. (snap)
He snapped at a flea. (snap)
He snapped at a minnow. (snap)

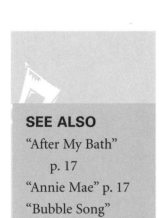

SEE ALSO
"After My Bath"
     p. 17
"Annie Mae" p. 17
"Bubble Song"
     p. 135
"Evan's Bath Song"
     p. 17

And he snapped at me. (snap)
He caught the mosquito. (clap)
He caught the flea. (clap)
He caught the minnow. (clap)
But he didn't catch me. (wave index finger as if saying no-no)

Three Tricky Turtles by Pam Schiller (Tune: Three Blind Mice)

Three pokey turtles.
Three pokey turtles.
See how they move.
See how they move.
They all decided to race a deer.
Their friends and family began to cheer.
The deer got beat by a trick I hear.
Three tricky turtles.
Three tricky turtles.

Literacy Activities

(Select one or two follow-up activities to do each time you sing a song or say a rhyme.)

Comprehension

1. Ask the children questions about the song. *What happened in the song? Who got bubbles in his throat? Who helped get the bubbles out of Tiny Tim's throat?*

Phonological Awareness

1. Help the children identify the rhyming pairs of words, such as "Tim/swim," "soap/throat," and "nurse/purse."

Letter Knowledge and Recognition

1. Write "Tiny Tim" on chart paper. Ask the children to identify the letters they recognize. *Which letters appear more than once?* Point out that Tiny Tim is an example of **alliteration**—both words begin with the same letter sound.

Print Awareness

1. Print "Tiny Tim" on chart paper. Say the chant, pointing out the left to right and top to bottom direction in which you are reading.

Learning Centers

Art (Bubble Art)

Mix prepared bubble mixture with powdered paint in a bowl. Encourage the children to blow bubbles onto their paper. When the bubbles pop, they leave a circular print. Or, let children dip bubble wrap (larger bubble size) in a tray of tempera paint, and then press the wrap onto a piece of paper to make a print.

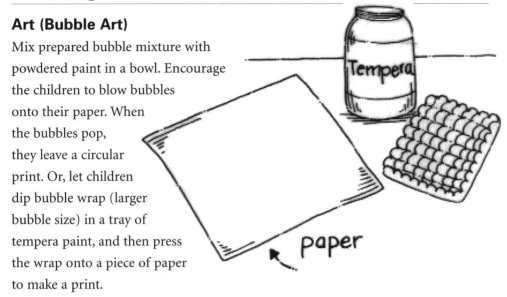

paper

Dramatic Play (Doctor and Nurse)

Provide a stuffed or plastic turtle and doctor and nurse props, e.g., a stethoscope, bandages, empty medicine bottles, towels, and so forth. Encourage the children to pretend to be nursing Tiny Tim. *When the patient is an animal, what is the doctor called?* Give the children the flannel board story and encourage them to retell the story.

Science (Turtle Photos)

Provide photos of turtles or, if available, borrow a live turtle for the day. Encourage the children to discuss the characteristics of turtles.

Writing (Tiny Tim)

Write "Tiny Tim" on several index cards. Invite the children to trace over the letters with a piece of soap.

Outdoor Play or Music and Movement Activity

1. Teach the children how to do the Turtle Rock. Have them lie on their back and then draw their legs and arms into their chest. Play some music and encourage the children to rock and roll on their backs. Be sure to do this activity on a soft surface.
2. Blow bubbles and encourage the children to chase them.
3. Sing along with "Tiny Tim the Turtle" (*Dr. Jean Sings Silly Songs* CD, Jean Feldman).

REFLECTIONS
Can you think of other animals that move slowly like a turtle?

Do turtles need lessons to know how to swim?

Tooty Ta

Tooty Ta

(suit actions to words)

Tooty ta, tooty ta,
Tooty ta, ta.

Thumbs up
Tooty ta, tooty ta,
Tooty ta, ta.

Elbows back
Tooty ta, tooty ta,
Tooty ta, ta.

Feet apart
Tooty ta, tooty ta,
Tooty ta, ta.

Knees together
Tooty ta, tooty ta,
Tooty ta, ta.

Bottoms up
Tooty ta, tooty ta,
Tooty ta, ta.

Tongue out
Tooty ta, tooty ta,
Tooty ta, ta.

Eyes shut
Tooty ta, tooty ta,
Tooty ta, ta.

Turn around
Tooty ta, tooty ta,
Tooty ta, ta.

(Beginning consonants can be changed to
any letter—"tooty ta" can be "mooty ma,"
etc.)

**THEME
CONNECTIONS**

Humor

Parts of the Body

Related Songs, Chants, and Rhymes

Dr. Knickerbocker

Dr. Knickerbocker, Knickerbocker, number nine, (clap and snap fingers to the beat)
We can get the rhythm most any old time.
So, let's get the rhythm in our hands—clap, clap. (clap hands)
Oh, we can get the rhythm in our hands—clap, clap. (clap hands)

…in our feet—stomp, stomp… (stomp feet)

…in our heads—ding, dong… (move head from side to side)

…in our hips—"hot dog!"… (wiggle hips)

…in our arms—"whoopee!"… (shake arms in the air)

…all over! (repeat all movements)

It's a Very Simple Dance to Do

Come on and do a dance with me.
It's just a little step or two.
I'll teach you how.
We'll start right now.
It's a very simple dance to do.

First you clap your hands. (clap three times)
Then stomp your feet, (stomp three times)
It's a very simple dance to do.

Wait, I forgot to tell you.
There's another little step or two.
Turn around (turn around)
And touch your toes. (touch your toes)
It's a very simple dance to do.

Clap your hands. (clap three times)
Stomp your feet. (stomp three times)
Turn around (turn around)
And touch your toes. (touch your toes)
It's a very simple dance to do.

Wait I forgot to tell you.
There's another little step or two.
Pull your ears (pull your ears)
And flap your arms. (flap your arms)
It's a very simple dance to do.

Clap your hands. (clap hands)
Stomp your feet. (stomp feet)
Turn around (turn around)
And touch your toes. (touch your toes)
Pull your ears (pull ears)
And flap your arms. (flap arms)
It's a very simple dance to do.

Wait I forgot to tell you.
There's another step and then we're
through.
Stretch up high. (stretch up high)
All fall down. (fall down)
It's a very simple dance to do.

Clap your hands. (suit actions to words)
Stomp your feet.
Turn around
And touch your toes.
Pull your ears
And flap your arms.
Now stretch up high.
All fall down.
It's a very simple dance to do.

(repeat last chorus)

Literacy Activities

(Select one or two follow-up activities to do each time you sing a song or say a rhyme.)

Oral Language Development

1. Discuss the position words ("in," "out," "back," "up," and so on) used in the song. Have volunteers demonstrate the various positions.

2. Say the rhyme reversing the actions. Instead of "thumbs up" say, "Thumbs down." Instead of "elbows back" say, "Elbows forward." *How far can you go?*

Phonological Awareness

1. Substitute another consonant for "T" in "Tooty Ta." For example, "Tooty ta" can be "mooty ma," "rooty ra," or even "wooty wa." Point out the **alliterative** words. Circle the repetitive letters.

Letter Knowledge and Recognition

1. Print "Tooty Ta" on chart paper. Ask the children to identify the letter that they recognize. *Which letters appear more than once?*

Learning Centers

Dramatic Play (Funny Faces)

Encourage the children to make funny faces in the mirror. They can start with sticking out their tongue as suggested in the song. Make suggestions for other funny faces. Encourage the children to be creative. *What other faces can you make? What makes a funny face funny?*

Fine Motor (Thumb Wrestling)

Teach the children how to thumb wrestle. Show them how to hold hands leaving their thumbs exposed. Tell them on the count of three they should try to use their thumb to pin their opponent's thumb down. They may not be adept at this but they will have fun trying.

Games (Thumb Ring Toss)

Make rings from pipe cleaners. Have the children choose a partner. One child holds his or her thumb up while the second child sits across the table and tries to toss the pipe cleaner ring over his or her partner's thumb.

Writing (Tooty Ta)

Write "Tooty Ta" on chart paper. Invite the children to use their thumb to copy the words in a tray of sand. *Is it easy or difficult to use your thumb as a writing instrument?*

Outdoor Play or Music and Movement Activity

1. Invite the children to walk across the playground with a ball held between their knees. *How long does it take to cross the playground?*
2. Sing along with "Dr. Knickerbocker" (*Dr. Jean and Friends* CD, Jean Feldman) or "Tooty Ta" (*Dr. Jean and Friends* CD, Jean Feldman).

BRAIN CONNECTION

Humor is an excellent strategy to boost memory potential. The endorphins that are released when we laugh are memory enhancers.

REFLECTIONS

What makes "Tooty Ta" such a silly chant?

Which parts of the chant do you like the best?

Twinkle, Twinkle, Little Star

Twinkle, Twinkle, Little Star
(Tune: Traditional)

Twinkle, twinkle, little star,
How I wonder what you are.
Up above the world so high,
Like a diamond in the sky.
Twinkle, twinkle little star.
How I wonder what you are.

When the blazing sun is set,
And the grass with dew is wet,
Then you show your little light,
Twinkle, twinkle, all the night.

Then the traveler in the dark
Thanks you for your tiny spark.
How could he see where to go
If you did not twinkle so?

As your bright and tiny spark
Lights the traveler in the dark.
Though I know not what you are,
Twinkle, twinkle, little star.

Related Songs, Chants, and Rhymes

Little Drop of Dew (Tune: Traditional)

Little drop of dew
Like a gem you are.
I believe that you
Must have been a star.

When the day is light
On the grass you lie.
Tell me then at night
Are you in the sky?

Star Light, Star Bright

Star light, star bright,
First star I've seen tonight.
I wish I may, I wish I might,
Have this wish I wish tonight.

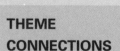

**THEME
CONNECTIONS**
Caring for the
    World/Ecology
Day and Night
Sun, Moon, Stars
Time of Day

Literacy Activities

(Select one or two follow-up activities to do each time you sing a song or say a rhyme.)

Oral Language Development

1. Discuss some of the words introduced in the song that may be new vocabulary for the children, i.e. "twinkle," "wonder," "diamond," and so forth.

2. Invite the children to sing the song using the word "tiny" instead of "little." Encourage them to use their voices to reflect the size of the star. Continue to sing the song, changing the description of the star and having children use their voices to reflect that description. For example, sing about a "great big star," a "jazzy star," and a "sleepy star." You may want to have the children clap out the syllables of the word "little" so that they understand that the word they use to describe the star should have two syllables.

Phonological Awareness

1. Invite the children to think of words that rhyme with star, for example, "bar," "car," "far," "mar," and "tar." You should also accept nonsense words.

Letter Knowledge and Recognition

1. Give each child a piece of blue construction paper to represent the sky. Write the word "star" on each piece of paper in large letters (2" to 3" high). Provide glue, rock salt (to represent stars), and tweezers. Encourage the children to glue the rock salt over the letters. When they are finished they will have written the word "star" with "stars" in the sky. If available, show the children pictures that illustrate how constellations often form shapes in the sky.

Learning Centers

Art (Night Skies)

Provide white felt "moons" (half moons, quarter moons, and full moons) and several white felt "stars." Encourage the children to create a night sky. Ask questions. *What things do you see in the sky at night? Which is larger: the moon or the stars? Is the moon a star? Is the moon always round? Do you ever see more than one moon in the sky?*

Blocks (Star Builders)

Challenge the children to think of a way that they can make a star shape out of blocks. If they seem stumped, suggest they use the triangle blocks. If you have pattern blocks, you might want to encourage the children to make star shapes using those before they use the regular building blocks.

Field Trip (Going to the Planetarium)

Take a trip to a planetarium.

Snack (An Apple a Day)

Serve apple halves. Encourage children to find the star shape in the center of their apple. Ask questions about the apples. *How does the outside skin feel? Are the apples crisp or soft? Do apples make a sound when you chew them?*

Outdoor Play or Music and Movement Activity

1. Try these music and movement ideas:

    ♪ Teach the children how to do the Texas Star square dance. *Why did someone name this dance the "Texas Star?"*

    ♪ Play "The Opera Singer" on *Singing, Moving and Learning,* Thomas Moore.

    ♪ Sing along with "Twinkle, Twinkle Little Star" (*Walt Disney Records: Children's Favorite Songs Vol. 1* CD).

REFLECTIONS

Name some ways we made stars today. Which activity did you enjoy most today? Why?

When we sang "Twinkle, Twinkle, Little Star" we changed our voices. Why did we do that? What kind of stars did we sing about?

The Weather Song

The Weather Song
(Tune: Clementine)

Sunny, sunny,   *Rainy, rainy,*
Sunny, sunny,   *Rainy, rainy,*
It is sunny in the sky.   *It is rainy in the sky.*
S-u-n-n-y, sunny   *R-a-i-n-y, rainy.*
It is sunny in the sky.   *It is rainy in the sky.*

Cloudy, cloudy,   *Foggy, foggy,*
Cloudy, cloudy,   *Foggy, foggy,*
It is cloudy in the sky. *It is foggy in the sky.*
C-l-o-u-d-y, cloudy   *F-o-g-g-y, foggy.*
It is cloudy in the sky. *It is foggy in the sky.*

Related Songs, Chants, and Rhymes

April Clouds

Two little clouds one April day, (hold both hands in fists)
Went sailing across the sky. (move fists from left to right)
They went so fast that they bumped their heads, (bump fists together)
And both began to cry. (point to eyes)

The big round sun came out and said, (make circle with arms)
"Oh, never mind, my dears,
I'll send all my sunbeams down (wiggle fingers downward like rain)
To dry your fallen tears."

Cold Fact by Dick Emmons

By the time he's suited
And scarved and booted
And mittened and capped
And zipped and snapped
And tucked and belted,
The snow has melted.

THEME CONNECTIONS

Emotions
Months of the Year
Movement
Opposites
Seasons
Self-Esteem
Sun, Moon, Stars
Weather

A Thunderstorm

Boom, bang, boom, bang,
Rumpety, lumpety, bump!
Zoom, zam, zoom, zam,
Clippity, clappity, clump!
Rustles and bustles,
And swishes and zings!
What wonderful sounds
A thunderstorm brings.

Whether the Weather

Whether the weather be fine,
Or whether the weather be not.
Whether the weather be cold,
Or whether the weather be hot.
We'll weather the weather,
Whatever the weather,
Whether we like it or not.

The Wind

Swoosh, swirl, swoosh, swirl,
Watch the leaves tumble and twirl.

SEE ALSO
"It's Raining" p. 171
"The Rain" p. 171
"Rain, Rain, Go
    Away" p. 171
"Raindrop Song"
    p. 170
"Side by Side"
    p. 149

Literacy Activities

(Select one or two follow-up activities to do each time you sing a song or say a rhyme.)

Oral Language Development

1. Discuss today's weather. Talk about all the other kinds of weather mentioned in the song. Ask questions. *How can you tell it is windy just by looking out the window? How can you tell it is cold without even going outside?* If weather photos are available, use them to stimulate discussion.

Letter Knowledge and Recognition

1. Write each weather word on chart paper. Let the children point out letters with which they are familiar. *What is the last letter in each word?* Say each of the words. *Can you hear that the last letter is the same in all the words?*

Learning Centers

Discovery (Wind Makers)

Provide several items that push and direct air (for example, a hand-held fan, squeeze bottles, straws, and basters) and several lightweight items (for example, feathers, straws, and tissue paper). Invite the children to explore using the air pushers to move the lightweight materials. *Which air pusher works best? Which item is easiest to move?*

Games (Raindrop Race)

Provide two eyedroppers, a cup of water, and a large cookie sheet. Have children choose a partner. Give each child an eyedropper. Show them how to use the eyedropper to pick up water. Place the cookie sheet in a sloping position. On the count of three, have the partners release a drop of water at the top of the cookie sheet. The drop that reaches the bottom of the cookie sheet first is the winner of the race. *What makes one drop fall faster than the other?*

Language (Under the Snow)

Write each of the weather words on index cards and laminate them. Tape them to a tabletop. Cover the tabletop with shaving cream and invite the children to explore the cream as if it were snow. As they uncover the various weather words, see if they are able to read them. If not, read the words to them.

Writing (All Kinds of Weather)

Write the weather words on large index cards. Encourage the children to trace the words on tracing paper or copy the words using magnetic letters. Some children will be able to write the words. Suggest that they write the words on index cards and add them to their Word Box (shoebox collection of words they can write).

Outdoor Play or Music and Movement Activity

1. Give each child a white streamer. Play some peaceful music and suggest they dance like clouds in a sky. Then provide gray or black streamers and play turbulent music. Suggest the children dance like storm clouds.
2. Sing along with "The Weather Song" (*Dr. Jean and Friends* CD, Jean Feldman).

BRAIN CONNECTION

Sunlight has an impact on our alertness, responsiveness, and moods. If we do not get enough sunlight, it slows the neuro-transmitters in the brain. Too many gray days take a toll. If you live in a part of the country that experiences dark winter months, you may want to investigate artificial lighting.

REFLECTIONS

What is your favorite kind of weather? Why?

What are some ways to warm your hands on a cold day?

The Wheels on the Bus

Wheels on the Bus
(Tune: Traditional)

The wheels on the bus go round and round. (move hands in circular motion)
Round and round, round and round.
The wheels on the bus go round and round,
All around the town. (extend arms up and out)

Additional verses:
The windshield wipers go swish, swish, swish...
    (sway hands back and forth)
The baby on the bus goes, "Wah,
    wah, wah"... (rub eyes)
The mommies on the bus
    say, shh, shh, shh ...
    (place index
    finger to
    mouth)

The people on the
    bus go up and down...
    (stand up, sit down)
The horn on the bus goes beep, beep, beep... (pretend to beep horn)
The money on the bus goes clink, clink, clink... (drop change in)
The driver on the bus says, "Move on back"... (hitchhiking movement)

Related Songs, Chants, and Rhymes

Little Hunk of Tin (Tune: I'm a Little Acorn Brown)

I'm a little hunk of tin. (cup hand as if holding something)
Nobody knows what shape I'm in. (hold hands to side palm up and shrug)
Got four wheels and a running board. (hold up four fingers)
I'm a four-door. (shake head yes)
I'm a Ford.

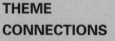

**THEME
CONNECTIONS**
Humor
Occupations
Things That Go
    Together
Travel/Transportation

SEE ALSO

"Barges" p. 175

"A Boy and a Girl in
a Little Canoe"
p. 176

"Row, Row, Row
Your Boat"
p. 175

Chorus:

Honk, honk. (pull ear)

Rattle, rattle. (shake head)

Crash, crash. (push chin)

Beep, beep. (push nose)

Repeat chorus twice

Literacy Activities

(Select one or two follow-up activities to do each time you sing a song or say a rhyme.)

Oral Language Development

1. Discuss riding on a bus. If any of the children have ridden on a bus, ask them to describe their experiences.
2. Add your own verses to the song, for example, "singers on the bus sing tra-la-la," "nappers on the bus go snort, snort, snort," and "teachers on the bus say, "Let's all sing.""

Print Awareness

1. Print the song on chart paper. Sing it while pointing out the left-to-right and top-to-bottom progression of the print.

Learning Centers

Art (Tire Track Designs)

Provide a tray of tempera paint, some small cars (or even better, buses), and some paper. Encourage the children to run the cars and/or buses through the paint and then across their paper in a variety of directions to create tire track designs.

Discovery (The Sound of Money)

Prepare several Sound Canisters. Fill small cans with sand, pebbles, paper clips, and pennies and tape them closed. Encourage the children to shake the various canisters to determine which one contains the pennies. Challenge them to describe the various sounds they hear as they shake each canister. *Does the money in the Sound Canister sound like the sound used for money in the song?*

Science (To Roll or Not to Roll)

Give the children items that are round and will roll, and some that are not round and won't roll. Provide an inclined plank and challenge the children to identify the items that will roll. Ask questions while they work. *What makes some things roll and others not roll? Can you tell before you test the item whether it is going to roll or not?*

Writing (Round and Round)

Write the word "round" in large letters on large index cards. Fill an empty, clean roll-on deodorant bottle with tempera paint and invite the children to roll over the letters with the paint.

Outdoor Play or Music and Movement Activity

1. Give the children "wheels" (circular pieces of cardboard). Encourage them to race their wheels.

2. Try these music and movement ideas:
    *   Sing along with an instrumental version of "The Wheels on the Bus" (*Twinkle, Twinkle Jazzy Star* CD, Thomas Moore).
    *   Sing along with "Wheels on the Bus" (*Walt Disney Records: Children's Favorite Songs Vol. 4* CD).

REFLECTIONS

How are buses and cars alike? How are they different?

What would happen if a bus had square wheels?

Where Is Thumbkin?

Where Is Thumbkin?
(Tune: Frère Jacques)

Where is thumbkin? (hands behind back)
Where is thumbkin?
Here I am. Here I am. (bring out right thumb, then left)
How are you today, sir? (bend right thumb)
Very well, I thank you. (bend left thumb)
Run away. Run away. (put right thumb behind back, then left thumb
    behind back)

Other verses:
Where is pointer?
Where is middle one?
Where is ring finger?
Where is pinky?
Where is the family?

Related Songs, Chants, and Rhymes

Dance, Thumbkin, Dance

Dance, Thumbkin, dance. (dance thumbs around, moving and bending them)
Dance, ye merrymen, everyone. (dance all fingers)
For Thumbkin, he can dance alone,
Thumbkin, he can dance alone.

Dance, Foreman, dance. (dance index fingers around, moving and bending them)
Dance, ye merrymen, everyone. (dance all fingers)
For Foreman, he can dance alone,
Foreman, he can dance alone.

Dance, Longman, dance. (dance middle fingers around, moving and bending them)
Dance, ye merrymen, everyone. (dance all fingers)
For Longman, he can dance alone,
Longman, he can dance alone.

THEME CONNECTIONS
Family
Friends
Manners
Movement
Parts of the Body

Dance, Ringman, dance. (dance ring fingers around—they won't bend alone)

Dance, ye merrymen, everyone. (dance all fingers)

For Ringman, he cannot dance alone,

Ringman, he cannot dance alone.

Dance, Littleman, dance. (dance little fingers around, moving and bending them)

Dance, ye merrymen, everyone. (dance all fingers)

For Littleman, he can dance alone,

Littleman, he can dance alone.

SEE ALSO

"Open, Shut Them" p. 160

"These Little Hands of Mine" p. 161

Hello, Good Friends

Hello, good friends.

How do you do?

Say your name,

And we'll clap for you.

(point to a child and have him or her state his or her name; clap)

Where Is A?

Where is A? (place hands behind back)

Where is A?

Here I am. Here I am. (bring right hand out showing the manual alphabet letter "A"; bring the left hand out showing the same letter)

How are you today, A? (bend right thumb)

Very well, I thank you. (bend left thumb)

Run away. Run away. (put right thumb behind back, then left thumb behind back)

(Continue the song with several letters.)

 The American Manual Alphabet uses finger positions that correspond to the letters of the alphabet to spell out words and names (sign language). The Internet is a great source for printable charts of the alphabet (www.iidc.indiana.edu/cedir/kidsweb/amachart.html or www.arethasplace.com/manabc.html).

Literacy Activities

(Select one or two follow-up activities to do each time you sing a song or say a rhyme.)

Oral Language Development

1. Teach the children to say, "How are you?" in Spanish (*"Como esta usted?"*). Teach them to respond, *"Muy bien, gracias."*

2. Talk with the children about the actual names for each of the fingers: thumb, index finger, middle finger, ring finger, and little finger (or pinky).

3. Discuss the pattern of question/answer used in the song. Brainstorm a list of questions that are often asked. For example,

How are you?	What time is it?
What are you doing?	What is your name?
How old are you?	

If the children are ready, you may want to mention that questions generally begin with specific words: who, what, when, where, why, and how.

Learning Centers

Dramatic Play (Finger Puppets)

Help the children draw faces on their fingers to make "puppets." Encourage them to use the puppets to act out "Where Is Thumbkin?"

Fine Motor (Thumb Wrestling)

Teach the children how to thumb wrestle. Have them clasp hands with thumbs facing up. Count to three and challenge each child to clamp down on her opponent's thumb. Discuss being gentle before starting the game.

Science (Looking for Details)

Provide magnifying glasses and an ink pad. Encourage the children to make fingerprints and then look at them closely with the magnifying glass. *Can you see the little lines?*

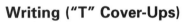

Writing ("T" Cover-Ups)

Print the letter "T" on index cards. Provide an ink pad and encourage the children to cover the "T" with thumbprints. Point out that thumb begins with the letter "T".

Outdoor Play or Music and Movement Activity

1. Play Thumbkin Says as you would Simon Says. Choose one child to be Thumbkin. All the other children stand side-by-side in a line facing Thumbkin. The child playing Thumbkin gives the other children orders to carry out, but only when the orders follow the phrase "Thumbkin says..." (e.g., "Thumbkin says touch your nose"). If a child follows an order that Thumbkin did not say (e.g., "Touch your nose"), then he is out and must sit down. The last child standing becomes the new Thumbkin for the next round.

2. Play an instrumental version of "Where Is Thumbkin?" (*Twinkle, Twinkle, Jazzy Star* CD, Thomas Moore) or sing along with "Where Is Thumbkin?" (*Where Is Thumbkin?* CD, Kimbo).

REFLECTIONS

Thumbkin is a funny name for our thumb. Can you think of another funny name we could call our thumb? (Thumbelina, Thumbie, Thumbco, Thummy). Can you think of a word that rhymes with thumb?

What are some things we use our thumbs for?

Appendix

Theme Chart

Theme	Songs	Chants/Rhymes
Me	Do Your Ears Hang Low? Head, Shoulders, Knees, and Toes I Have Something in My Pocket I Love the Mountains I Wish I Were If You're Happy and You Know It My Hand on My Head Open, Shut Them This Little Light of Mine Where Is Thumbkin?	Clap Your Hands Head, Shoulders, Baby I Can, You Can I Wish I Had a Dinosaur My Body Talks Say and Touch Soft Touches Sometimes These Little Hands of Mine Tooty Ta Uniquely Me Warm-Up Chant Where Do You Wear Your Ears?
Families	Baby Bumblebee Be Kind to Your Web-Footed Friends A Bicycle Built for Two Catalina Magnalina Farmer in the Dell Hush, Little Baby Miss Mary Mack There Once Were Three Brown Bears Over the River and Through the Woods Rhyme Time Rockabye, Baby She'll Be Comin' 'Round the Mountain Ten in the Bed Three Bears Rap	Family Fun Five Little Monkeys Grandpa's (or Grandma's) Glasses Hey! My Name Is Joe! Jack and Jill The Old Lady in the Shoe
Friends	For He's a Jolly Good Fellow Good Morning to You! Hello, Good Friends Make New Friends The More We Get Together My Bonnie Lies Over the Ocean Polly Wolly Doodle Say, Say, My Playmate Side by Side Skidamrink There's a Hole in the Bucket This Is Austin	Jack and Jill

Theme	Songs	Chants/Rhymes
Pets	Bingo Fiddle-I-Fee Fido My Dog Rags Where, Oh, Where, Has My Little Dog Gone? Whose Dog Are Thou?	Old Gray Cat Old Mother Hubbard
Seasons	Caps, Mittens, Shoes, and Socks Down by the Bay Gray Squirrel I'm a Little Acorn Brown Jingle Bells Over the River and Through the Woods The Weather Song	April Clouds Chocolate Rhyme Cold Fact Mighty Fine Turkey Whether the Weather

Colors	A Tisket, A Tasket
	America the Beautiful
	Catalina Magnalina
	The Color Song
	Farm Colors
	Gray Squirrel
	The Green Grass Grew All Around
	If You're Happy and You Know It
	The Iguana in Lavender Socks
	I'm a Little Acorn Brown
	Lavender's Blue
	Miss Mary Mack
		Color Chants
		  I Like Red
		  I Like Yellow
		  I Like Blue
		  I Like Green
		Great Green Gobs
		Little Boy Blue
		Little Red Apple

Holidays/ Celebrations	Five Fat Turkeys Jack-O-Lantern Jingle Bells Over the River and Through the Woods	Five Little Pumpkins Five Waiting Pumpkins Mighty Fine Turkey
Sound and Movement	Are You Sleeping? The Ants Go Marching Barges A Boy and a Girl in a Little Canoe Did You Ever See a Lassie? Doodle-li-do The Grand Old Duke of York Johnny Works With One Hammer The Little Ants Little Hunk of Tin Old Gray Cat Old MacDonald Has a Band	Big Brass Band Dance, Thumbkin, Dance Floppy Rag Doll Hey! My Name Is Joe It's a Simple Dance to Do Jack-in-the-Box The Rain A Thunderstorm Tooty Ta The Wind

Theme	Songs	Chants/Rhymes
Sound and Movement (cont'd.)	Open, Shut Them Row, Row, Row Your Boat Ten in the Bed This Old Man This Old Man Is Rockin' On The Wheels on the Bus	
Music	Doodle-li-do MacNamara's Band Old MacDonald Has a Band This Old Man Is Rockin' On	Big Bass Drum Three Bears Rap
Animals	A-Hunting We Will Go Animal Fair Annie Mae Be Kind to Your Web-Footed Friends Bingo Birdie, Birdie, Where Is Your Nest? Down by the Bay Farmer in the Dell Fiddle-I-Fee Fido Five Little Ducks Five Little Fishes Swimming in the Sea Five Little Speckled Frogs Frog Went A-Courtin' Grey Squirrel Hanky Panky Hickory Dickory Dock Home on the Range Little Ducky Duddle Little Skunk's Hole Mary Had a Little Lamb My Dog Rags Old MacDonald Had a Farm One Little Duck Over in the Meadow Over the River and Through the Woods She'll Be Comin' 'Round the Mountain Six White Ducks The Bear Went Over the Mountain There's a Hole in the Middle of the Sea Three Blind Mice Three Tricky Turtles Three White Mice Tiny Tim Where, Oh, Where Has My Little Dog Gone? Whose Dog Are Thou?	Downy Duck Five Little Monkeys Going on a Bear Hunt Going on a Safari Going on a Whale Watch Hey, Diddle Diddle Little Boy Blue Old Gray Cat Old Mother Hubbard The Owl and the Pussy Cat The Squirrel There Once Was a Turtle There Was a Crooked Man This Little Piggy To Market, To Market

Theme	Songs	Chants/Rhymes
Insects	The Ants Go Marching Baby Bumblebee Down by the Bay Fuzzy Caterpillar The Insect Song Itsy Bitsy Spider Little Ant's Hill Little Ants Little Bee's Hive Mosquitoes Shoo Fly	Anthill The Caterpillar Hickey Picky Bumblebee Little Miss Muffet Metamorphosis Pretty Butterfly There Once Was a Turtle
Day and Night	Are You Sleeping? Hush Little Baby It's Raining Lazy Mary Little Drop of Dew Mister Moon Mister Sun Rockabye Baby Skidamarink Twinkle, Twinkle, Little Star	Star Light, Star Bright Wynken, Blynken, and Nod
Nursery Rhymes	Mary Had a Little Lamb Nursery Rhyme Rap Twinkle, Twinkle, Little Star	Hey, Diddle, Diddle Hickory Dickory Dock Humpty Dumpty Little Boy Blue Little Miss Muffet Old Mother Hubbard There Was an Old Woman Who Lived in a Shoe This Little Piggy To Market, To Market
Food	Apples and Bananas The Donut Song Do You Know the Muffin Man? Found a Peanut Johnny Appleseed Just Plant a Watermelon Oats, Peas, Beans, and Barley The Raindrop Song She'll Be Comin' 'Round the Mountain Take Me Out to the Ball Game	Apples and Bananas Chant Chocolate Rhyme Hot Cross Buns! The Ice Cream Chant Little Miss Muffet Little Red Apple My Apple Old Mother Hubbard Pat-A-Cake Peanut Butter Peas Porridge Hot Rima de chocolate Who Stole the Cookies From the Cookie Jar?

Theme	Songs	Chants/Rhymes
Weather	The Ants Go Marching Be Kind to Your Web-Footed Friends It's Raining Itsy Bitsy Spider Jingle Bells Lazy Mary Over the River and Through the Woods Rain, Rain Go Away The Raindrop Song The Weather Song	April Clouds Cold Fact The Rain A Thunderstorm Whether the Weather The Wind
Farms	Bingo Farm Colors Farmer in the Dell Fiddle-I-Fee Five Little Ducks Old MacDonald Had a Farm Three Blind Mice Three White Mice	Five Waiting Pumpkins
Growing Things	Are You Growing? The Earth Is Our Home Great Green Gobs The Green Grass Grew All Around Just Plant a Watermelon Oats, Peas, Beans, and Barley Grow Under the Spreading Chestnut Tree	Peanut Butter Tiny Seeds
Counting/ Numbers	The Ants Go Marching Five Fat Turkeys Five Friends Dancing in a Line Five Little Ducks Five Little Fishes Swimming in the Sea Five Little Speckled Frogs Johnny Works With One Hammer Over in the Meadow Six White Ducks This Old Man	Chocolate Rhyme Counting Rhyme Five Little Monkeys Five Little Pumpkins Five Waiting Pumpkins Head, Shoulders, Baby One, Two Buckle My Shoe One Potato, Two Potato Rima de Chocolate Ten in the Bed
Funny People	Annie Mae Catalina Magnalina Michael Finnegan Miss Mary Mack Polly Wolly Doodle Risseldy, Rosseldy	There Was a Crooked Man

Theme	Songs	Chants/Rhymes
Travel/ Transportation	Barges A Boy and a Girl in a Little Canoe Little Hunk of Tin Over the River and Through the Woods Row, Row, Row Your Boat She'll Be Comin' 'Round the Mountain This Is the Way We Pack for Travel The Wheels on the Bus	Clickety Clack I'm a Little Choo Choo
Way Out West	Dusty Home on the Range I'm a Texas Star Trigger	
Traditional Tales	Over the River and Through the Woods The Three Bears Rap There Once Were Three Brown Bears	The Giant Stomp
Caring for Our World/Ecology	America the Beautiful The Ash Grove The Earth Is My Home I Love the Mountains Johnny Appleseed Little Drop of Dew Mister Moon Mister Sun Twinkle, Twinkle, Little Star	I Love the Ocean

Rebus Recipes

Frogs on a Log (Five Little Speckled Frogs)

1. Cut celery into 3" strips.
2. Place peanut butter in the opening of the celery.
3. Cut grapes in half lengthwise.
4. Place 3 or 4 grape halves on top of the peanut butter to represent ants.

1. Cut celery into 3" strips.

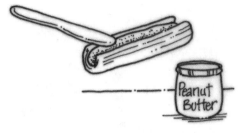

2. Place peanut butter in the opening of the celery.

3. Cut grapes in half lengthwise.

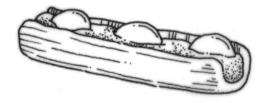

4. Place 3 or 4 grape halves on top of the peanut butter to represent ants.

Hot Chocolate (Chocolate Rhyme)

1. Place 1 tablespoon of chocolate syrup in a cup of milk.
2. Stir.
3. Heat in the microwave or stovetop until warm (adult only).
4. Add marshmallows.

1. Place 1 tablespoon of chocolate syrup in a cup of milk.

2. Stir.

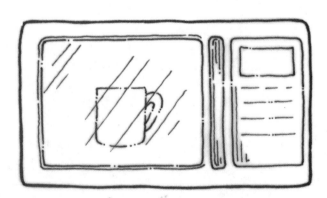

3. Heat in the microwave or stove top till warm. (adult only.)

4. Add marshmallows.

Gelatin Jigglers

1. Mix flavored gelatin with half the amount of water suggested on the box.
2. Chill.
3. Cut into shapes or use a cookie cutter to cut.

1 Mix flavored gelatin with half the amount of water suggested on the box

2. Chill.

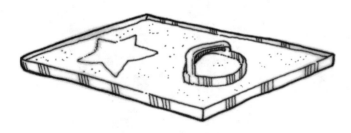

3. Cut into shapes or use a cookie cutter to cut.

Patterns

Alphabet Letter Patterns

(Alphabet Forwards and Backward and Over the River and Through the Woods)

Aa	Bb	Cc
Dd	Ee	Ff
Gg	Hh	Ii

Alphabet Letter Patterns

(Alphabet Forwards and Backward and Over the River and Through the Woods)

Jj	**Kk**	**Ll**
Mm	**Nn**	**Oo**
Pp	**Qq**	**Rr**

Alphabet Letter Patterns

(Alphabet Forwards and Backward and Over the River and Through the Woods)

Ss	**Tt**	**Uu**
Vv	**Ww**	**Xx**
Yy	**Zz**	

Caterpillar/butterfly puppet (Fuzzy Caterpillar)

Turn a brown or black sock inside out. Glue or sew two wiggle eyes onto the toe of the sock. Then turn the sock right side out, glue or sew two wiggle eyes on the toe and two felt wings midway up the sock.

butterfly

Engine pattern

Katy pattern (K-K-Katy)

Alphabet Train pattern (Alphabet Forwards and Backward)

Alphabet Train pattern (Alphabet Forwards and Backward)

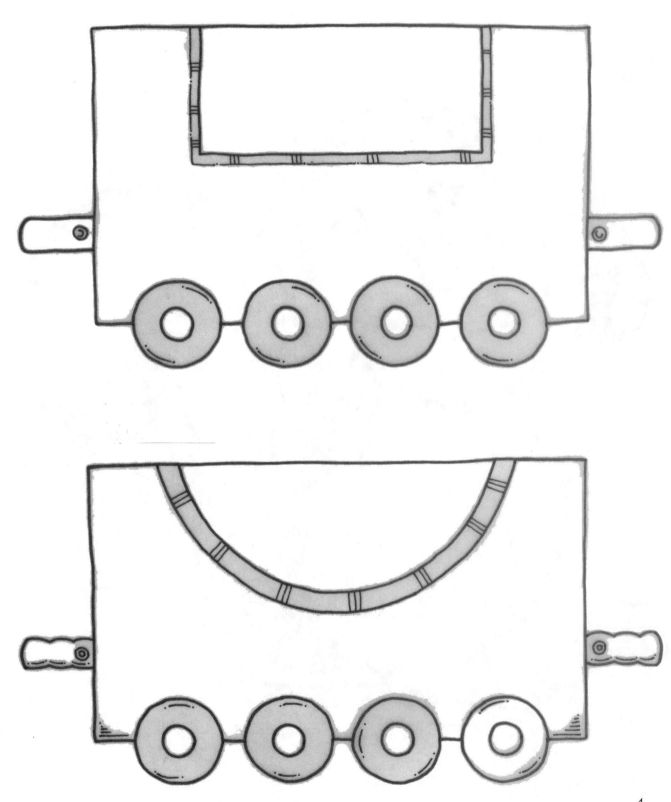

Squirrel pattern (Gray Squirrel)

American Sign Language Signs

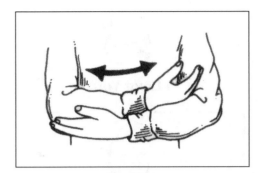

Baby

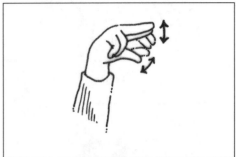

Duck

Bear

Father

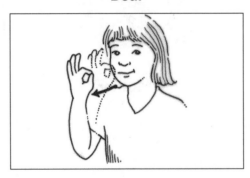

Cat

Fish

Dog

Flowers

Frog

I Love You

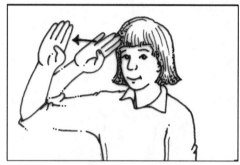

Hello, Friend

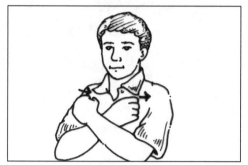

Love

Horse

Mother

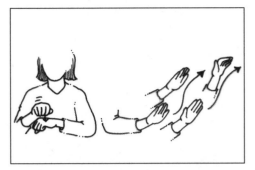

Mountains

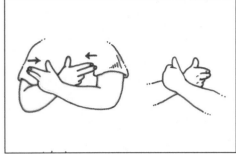

Rabbit

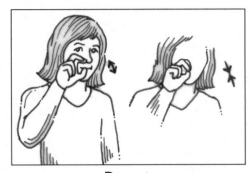

Parrot

Squirrel

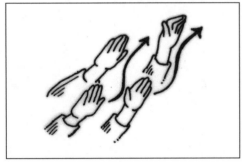

Hills

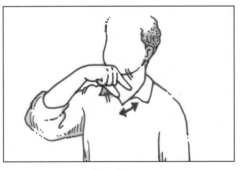

Turkey

Music Websites

www.kididdles.com

www.judyanddavid.com

www.usscouts.org

www.drthomasmoore.com

www.mamalisa.com

www.theteachersguide.com

www.niehs.nih.gov/kids/musicchild.htm

Indexes

Theme Index

Songs

Game Index

B

Beanbag Walk, 95

Bear Hunt, 80

Bubble Trouble, 174

Button Toss, 95

C

Catalina Says, 38

Chicken Feather Race, 159

Cooperative Musical Marshmallows, 42

D

Ding, Ding, Dong, 28

Dog and Bone, 103

Dog Bowl Toss, 102

Don't Let the Ball Fall,1 74

Doodle, Doodle, Do, 54

Drop the Heart, 183

Drop the Nut, 86

Drop the Peanut, 169

Duck, Duck, Goose, 62, 139

E

Egg Races, 106

F

Farmer in the Dell, 97, 157, 159

Feed the Dog, 34

Fish, 66

Flashlight Tag, 195

Freeze, 111

Frog Jumps, 69

Fruit Salad, 25

G

Grandmother, May I? 166

H

Hog, Hog, Pig, 197

Hopscotch, 66

Horseshoes, 123

K

Katy Puzzles, 136

L

Leap Frog, 72

M

Matching, 22, 25, 28, 201

Mice Maze, 97

Motorboat, Motorboat, 177

N

Name Game, 174

P

Peanut Roll, 169

Pick Up Sticks, 177

Pin the Tail on the Squirrel, 86

Possum, 109

Pumpkin Relay Race, 134

R

Raindrop Race, 216

Rolling Home, 201

Roly Poly Races, 188

S

Scrabble, 174

Shadow Tag, 147

Simon Says, 155

Skunk Hole Miniature Golf, 142

T

Thumb Ring Toss, 210

Thumb Wrestling, 210, 222

Thumbkin Says, 222

Tic-Tac-Toe, 150

Toss a Match, 134

Tummy Ticklers, 151

Turkey Hunt, 59

W

Whale Tail, 57

Which Hand? 162

Who Stole the Cookies? 48

Who's Got the Button? 95

General Index

Where is Thumbkin?

500 Activities to Use with Songs You Already Know

Pam Schiller and Thomas Moore

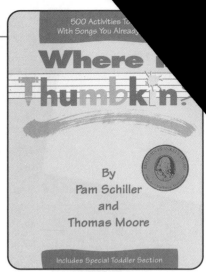

Sing over 200 familiar songs and learn new words set to familiar tunes. Organized by month, with a special sectin just for toddlers, this book provides easy, song-related activities that span the curriculum in areas such as math, art, and language. 256 pages. 1993.

ISBN 0-87659-164-0 / Gryphon House / 13156

The Complete Resource Book

An Early Childhood Curriculum
Pam Schiller

The Complete Resource Book is an absolute must-have book for every teacher. Offering a complete plan for every day of the year, this is an excellent reference book for responding to children's specific interests. Each daily plan contains:

- circle time activities
- music and movement activities
- suggested books
- six learning center ideas

The appendix, jam-packed with songs, recipes, and games is almost a book in itself. *The Complete Resrouce Book* is like a master teacher working at your side, offering guidance and inspiration all year long. 463 pages. 1998.

ISBN 0-87659-195-0 / Gryphon House / 15327